THE SCOTTISH OFFICE CENTRAL RESEARCH UNIT

Social Work
Research Findings No. 17

Social Work and Criminal Justice:
Parole Board Decision-Making

Lesley McAra

National Objectives and Standards for Social Work Services in the Criminal Justice System and the 100% funding initiative ('the policy') were introduced in 1991[1] in order to secure the provision of services which have the confidence of both criminal justice decision-makers and the wider public. This study is part of the social research programme designed to evaluate policy implementation.   It examines the impact of the policy on parole board decision-making.

Main findings

■ The Parole Board's expectations of social work parole reports were consistent with the National Standards but they indicated that they were less satisfied with the overall standard of home circumstance reports (HCRs) than prison social work reports.

■ Although none of the prison social work reports or HCRs in the study samples fully met the National Standards requirements,   social workers indicated that they did not always have access to the information required by the Standards.

■ Parole Board members commented that they lacked information about the content and process of parole supervision.

■ For most cases, change during time spent in custody rather than the quality of community-based services, was a key factor in Parole Board decision-making. This limits the impact of the policy on encouraging earlier release on licence by improving the quality of community-based social work supervision.

---

1 National Standards for Community Service had been introduced in 1989.

Introduction

The National Objectives and Standards (the Standards, 1991) set out a framework within which local authorities are required to provide social work services where costs are met by the 100 per cent funding initiative (initially social enquiry reports and associated court services, community service, probation, parole and other aspects of throughcare).

Prior to the development of the Standards, local authorities had to fund most social work services out of their general income. Criminal justice services were, therefore, in competition for resources with other local authority services and as a result were not always of sufficient quantity and quality to meet the requirements of the courts.

The main aims of the policy are:

- to reduce the use of custody by increasing the availability, improving the quality and targeting the use of community-based court disposals on those most at risk of custody, especially young offenders;

- to enable offenders to address their offending behaviour and make a successful adjustment to law-abiding life.

The purpose of this study was to examine the impact of policy implemention on parole board decision-making.

Four social work authorities were selected for study to reflect areas with urban centres, those which were predominantly rural and to represent both specialist and more generic forms of organising social work criminal justice services.

Findings are based on: observation of six Parole Board meetings in 1994; a sample of 68 prison social work reports and 63 home circumstances reports; semi-structured interviews conducted in 1995 with four members of the Parole Board for Scotland; interviews with one prison social worker and a group of community-based social workers from each of the four study sites.

Quality of reports

Interviewee responses indicated a high level of correspondence between the Parole Board's (the Board) expectations of social work parole reports and the requirements of the Standards.

A key concern of the Board was that the authors of prison social work reports and HCRs should collaborate in the preparation of reports.

While Parole Board interviewees were generally satisfied with prison social work reports, they were less satisfied with the overall standard of home circumstance reports. However, the information provided in the prison social work reports and HCRs in the report sample suggests that the Board does not always receive reports which fully meet its expectations.

Prison and community-based social work interviewees indicated that they did not always have access to information which would enable them to make the types of assessment required by the Standards. Most found it difficult to access verified information about the prisoner's criminal history and the nature of the current offence. This created difficulties when making assessments of risk of reoffending.

Availability and Quality of Services

Community-based services

Parole Board and social work interviewees considered that implementation of the Standards had resulted in an increase in services for which there was a high demand, especially addiction counselling. Other services, for which demand was relatively low, were markedly less well developed, in particular supervised and supported accommodation and services for mentally disturbed offenders.

Parole Board members commented that they lacked information about the content and process of community supervision. This made it difficult for them to assess whether policy implementation had resulted in improved quality of supervision.

Prison-based services

A general view of both Parole Board and social work interviewees was that prison social work services had improved since the implementation of 'Continuity Through Co-operation', a national framework of policy and practice guidance for social work in prisons, (Scottish Prisons Service/Social Work Services Group, 1989). Social workers were now undertaking more offence-focused work. Nevertheless, interviewees considered that there were variations in the range and quality of social work services in different prison establishments.

The uneven nature of services was attributed to poor service planning on the part of some local authorities and under-resourcing.

Impact on decision-making

The quality of community-based social work services did not feature amongst the principal factors which the Board took into account when making decisions on the majority of cases. This limits the impact of a policy aimed at encouraging earlier release on licence by improving the quality of statutory supervision.

For determinate sentence cases, risk of reoffending was the main factor which the Board took into consideration. For indeterminate sentence prisoners, the key focus of decision-making was progress in custody.

The Board's focus on change during time spent in custody, highlights the scope for high quality and effective prison-based social work services to impact positively on parole decisions. Parole Board interviewees considered that the effectiveness of such services was dependent both on the prisoner's motivation to address problems and the availability of a network of relevant services supplied by other specialist agencies.

Conclusion

Throughcare services were identified at phase one of the research programme as being the most poorly developed element of social work criminal justice services. The findings of this study indicate that the aspects of throughcare which impact on parole decision-making are still unevenly developed.

The study was carried out by the Centre for Law and Society at Edinburgh University as part of the programme of research to evaluate social work criminal justice policy. The research programme was conducted by The Scottish Office Central Research Unit in collaboration with the Social Work Research Centre at Stirling University and with Edinburgh University. It was funded by the Home Department of The Scottish Office.

Social Work and Criminal Justice Volume 5: 'Parole Board Decision-Making'; the report of the research programme summarised in this Research Findings is published by The Stationery Office. It may be purchased from The Stationery Office, price £14 per copy.

Reports of Individual Studies on this programme are also available:
Social Work and Criminal Justice Volume 1: 'The Impact of Policy'.
Social Work and Criminal Justice Volume 2: 'Early Arrangements'.
Social Work and Criminal Justice Volume 3: 'The National and Local Context'.
Social Work and Criminal Justice Volume 4: 'Sentencer Decision-Making'. ·
Social Work and Criminal Justice Volume 6: 'Probation'.
Social Work and Criminal Justice Volume 7: 'Community-Based Throughcare'.

Cheques should be made payable to The Stationery Office and addressed to:

The Stationery Office Ltd, Mail Order Department, 21 South Gyle Crescent, Edinburgh, EH12 9EB. Telephone: 0131-479-3141 or Fax 0131-479-3142.

The following Research Findings for other studies on this programme are also available:

Findings 13: 'The Impact of Policy'
Findings 14: 'Early Arrangements'.
Findings 15: 'The National and Local Context'.
Findings 16: 'Sentencer Decision-Making'.
Findings 18: 'Probation'.
Findings 19: 'Community-Based Throughcare'.
Research Findings may be photocopied, or further copies may be obtained from:

The Scottish Office Central Research Unit

Room 53

James Craig Walk

Edinburgh EH1 3BA

or

Telephone: 0131-244-5397

Fax: 0131-244-5393

THE SCOTTISH OFFICE

Designed and produced on behalf of The Scottish Office by The Stationery Office J16005 1/98

ISBN 0-7480-6663-2

9 780748 066636

SOCIAL WORK AND CRIMINAL JUSTICE:

VOLUME 5

PAROLE BOARD DECISION MAKING

Lesley McAra

Centre for Law and Society
University of Edinburgh

THE SCOTTISH OFFICE CENTRAL RESEARCH UNIT
1998

ACKNOWLEDGEMENTS

I am indebted to the members of the Parole Board for Scotland who kindly agreed to allow their work to be observed. Particular thanks are due to the Parole Board members, prison and community based social workers who agreed to be interviewed as part of the study.

I would like to acknowledge the advice and support received from The Scottish Office Home Department, in particular from Dr Jacqueline Tombs and Dr Fiona Paterson of the Central Research Unit.

Special thanks are due to Ms Liz Levy, Research Officer in the Central Research Unit, who coded the data, undertook some preliminary analysis of the recall data and assisted with the proof-checking. Particular thanks are also due to Ms Monica Barry of the Social Work Research Centre, University of Stirling, who checked proofs of the final drafts of the report.

Lesley McAra
1998

SOCIAL WORK AND CRIMINAL JUSTICE
RESEARCH PROGRAMME REPORTS

Paterson, F. and Tombs, J. (1998) Social Work and Criminal Justice: Volume 1 -

The Impact of Policy. The Stationery Office.

Phase One:

McAra, L. (1998) Social Work and Criminal Justice: Volume 2 -

Early Arrangements. The Stationery Office.

Phase Two:

Brown, L., Levy, L. Social Work and Criminal Justice: Volume 3 -

and McIvor, G. (1998) *The National and Local Context.* The Stationery Office.

Brown, L., Levy, L. (1998) Social Work and Criminal Justice: Volume 4 -

Sentencer Decision Making. The Stationery Office.

McAra, L. (1998a) Social Work and Criminal Justice: Volume 5 -

Parole Board Decision Making. The Stationery Office.

McIvor, G. and Social Work and Criminal Justice: Volume 6 -

Barry, M. (1998) *Probation.* The Stationery Office.

McIvor, G. and Social Work and Criminal Justice: Volume 7 -

Barry, M. (1998a) *Community Based Throughcare.* The Stationery Office.

CONTENTS

SUMMARY

INTRODUCTION

The Policy

In Scotland, statutory social work services to offenders and their families are provided by the local authority social work departments. Since April 1991, The Scottish Office has reimbursed to social work departments the full costs of providing a range of statutory social work services in the criminal justice system. National Objectives and Standards (the National Standards) were introduced by the Social Work Services Group of the Scottish Office (SWSG) to coincide with the introduction of the funding initiative.

The National Standards and the funding initiative cover: social enquiry reports; court social work services; probation; community service; and certain specified elements of throughcare services (namely social work parole reports and the supervision of offenders on release from prison). Since 1991 the initiative has been extended to supervised release orders, bail information and accommodation schemes, and supervised attendance order schemes (the latter two schemes are not yet available on a national basis).

The main aims of the Government's policy are:

- to reduce the use of custody by increasing the availability, improving the quality and targeting the use of community based court disposals and throughcare services on those most at risk of custody, especially young adult repeat offenders;

- to enable offenders to address their offending behaviour and make a successful adjustment to law abiding life.

Background to the Research

Central Government's review and evaluation of implementation of the funding initiative and the National Standards involves a programme of inspection by Social Work Services Inspectorate, interpretation of statistics and a programme of research.

The research programme examines progress towards policy objectives. Four sheriff court areas each in separate social work authorities, were selected as study sites for Phase Two of the research programme to reflect areas of both high and low population density and to represent both specialist and more generic forms of organising social work criminal justice services. The names of the four areas have been anonymised in reports and are referred to as Scott, Wallace, Burns and Bruce.

Aims and Methods

The present study examines the impact of arrangements for implementing the policy on Parole Board decision making including the impact of: social work parole reports; the quality of prison and community based social work services; and liaison arrangements.

The research is based on: observation of six Parole Board meetings held between January and March 1994; detailed analysis of all cases considered at the meetings (311 cases which are representative of the range of cases with which the Board deals); analysis of a sample of 68 prison social work reports and 63 home circumstances reports, drawn from the parole dossiers of cases considered at the meetings from each of four prison units (one prison unit was selected from each study site to reflect a range of units); semi-structured interviews with four members of the Parole Board for Scotland and four prison social workers; and a group interview conducted with community based social workers from each study site.

SOCIAL WORK PAROLE REPORTS AND DECISION MAKING

Information Requirements of the Board

Parole Board interviewee responses indicate that there was a high level of correspondence between the Parole Board's expectations of both prison social work and home circumstances reports and the requirements of the National Standards. A key concern of the Board was that the authors of prison social work and home circumstances reports should collaborate over the preparation of reports and that the two social work reports should provide a seamless web of information in respect of release plans and risk assessments.

All but one of the Parole Board interviewees were generally satisfied with the prison social work reports which they received. However, interviewees considered that the overall quality of home circumstances reports was less good, with two Parole Board interviewees commenting that home circumstances reports were often cursory, giving little indication that they were based on verified sources of information or that they had been prepared collaboratively with the author of the prison social work report.

Quality of Information in Reports

The information provided in both prison social work and home circumstances reports in the sample suggests that the Board does not always receive reports which fully meets its requirements. None of the reports in the sample fully met the National Standards and only 27 per cent of prison social work reports and 21 per cent of home circumstances reports indicated that they had been prepared on a collaborative basis.

Prison social work reports mainly indicated and assessed: the prisoner's personal circumstances; their response to imprisonment; and attitude towards the offence. Less well covered were the prisoner's attitude towards their sentence and attitudes towards release plans. Just over one half (35) of prison social work reports included an assessment of risk of re-offending.

Areas well covered in home circumstances reports were: background information, especially in relation to accommodation; family attitudes towards the prisoner and the environment to which the prisoner was to return. However, less than half the reports indicated and assessed: the prisoner's overall level of needs; the suitability of specialist resources to meet those needs; family attitude towards social work supervision; an assessment of risk factors.

Social Work Views on Reports

Social work interviewee responses highlight a number of reasons as to why reports may fall short of National Standards' requirements. Both prison and community based social work interviewees indicated that they did not always have access to information which would enable them to make the types of assessment required by the National Standards. Most found it difficult to access verified information about the prisoner's criminal history and the nature of the current offence and this created difficulties when making assessments of risk of re-offending. Prison social work interviewee responses also indicate that workloads may have impacted adversely on the extent to which they could implement the Standards.

Both prison and community based social workers identified elements of reports for which each considered that the other should take lead responsibility, in particular the development of release plans. (The National Standards require both prison social work and home circumstances reports to indicate the suitability of specialist resources and programmes in the community.) Prison social workers did not consider that they were best placed to assess the suitability of community based resources for the prisoner whereas community based social workers did not consider that they had sufficient information about the prisoner in order to assess their needs.

Use of Information: Decision making Practice

Although the quality of the report sample indicates that social workers do not always provide reports which meet the Board's expectations, poor quality of information was only an explicit factor in a minority of decisions during the observation period. Three decisions out of a total 290 relevant decisions (this excludes decisions made on cases referred for consideration of recall for which no social work reports were available) were deferred to await a more detailed prison social work report, with a further five deferred to give community based social workers time to prepare better researched reports.

SOCIAL WORK SERVICES AND DECISION MAKING

Specialist Community based Services

Both Parole Board and social work interviewees considered that National Standards implementation had resulted in the proliferation of certain community based services, especially addiction counselling. Other services were believed to be markedly less well developed, in particular supported accommodation and services for mentally disordered offenders. The observed decision making patterns indicate, however, that demand (as evidenced by the nature of additional requirements inserted into licences by the Board) for supported accommodation placements and psychological services was relatively low. By contrast services for which there was greatest demand (such as alcohol counselling) were the most prolific.

Supervision of Licencees

Parole Board interviewees commented that they often lacked information about the content and process of statutory supervision, particularly in relation to parolees. This made it difficult for them to assess whether policy implementation had resulted in improved quality of supervision. Nevertheless a general view was that quality of supervision was likely to impact on a licencee's willingness to adhere to their licence conditions. However, interviewees considered that there was little that social workers could do to prevent re-offending. This contrasts with the model of social work practice in the National Standards which is premised on the belief that supervision which provides the requisite balance of care and control can impact positively on offending behaviour.

Prison based Social Work Services

A general view of both Parole Board and prison social work interviewees was that prison social work services had improved since the implementation of *Continuity Through Co-operation* (a national framework of policy and practice guidance for social work in prisons, The Scottish Office Social Work Services Group/Scottish Prison Service 1989) with social workers now undertaking more offence focused work. Nevertheless interviewees still considered that there were variations in the range and quality of social work services in different prison establishments. Key gaps in services were identified as: relationship counselling, anger management counselling; and services for gamblers. The uneven nature of service provision was attributed to poor strategic planning on the part of some local authorities and to under-resourcing.

Both Parole Board and prison social work interviewees highlighted the need for prison units to develop a network of services, supplied by both social work and other specialist agencies. Where such a network existed, this was felt to enhance the effectiveness of the social work contribution.

Impact of Community based Services on Parole Board Decision making

Parole Board interviewees did not consider that arrangements for implementing the policy had impacted on their decision making practice. Both the interview and observation data confirm that the nature or quality of community based social work services did not feature amongst the principal factors which the Board took into account when making decisions in the majority of cases. This limits the impact of a policy aimed at encouraging earlier release on licence by improving the quality of statutory supervision.

Determinate Sentence Cases

For determinate sentence cases, risk of re-offending was the main factor which the Board took into account. Key indicators of risk were identified by Parole Board interviewees as: the nature and circumstances of the current offence; the number and pattern of previous convictions; the extent to which the offender had addressed their offending behaviour and any related problems; the level of support the offender would have on release; and plans for managing time in the community.

However the observed decision making patterns indicate that in the *majority* of cases where the Board considered that a prisoner had not made efforts to address their offending during time spent in custody, the Board attached *less weight* to constructive release plans in their assessment of re-offending risk. Where the Parole Board perceived a prisoner to be low risk they recommended them for parole or a forward release date. High risk prisoners by contrast were generally not released.

Analysis of the decision making patterns identified only 39 (18 per cent) out of 216 determinate sentence cases, for which there was evidence that social work services were an important consideration in the decision that was made. However, a high proportion of these cases was considered to be at a low risk of re-offending or had features which the Board confirmed in interview to be indicative of low risk, *in addition* to the identified social work resource. As cases with such low risk features were generally recommended for release, this suggests that the availability of social work services had a *contributory* but not necessarily a *pivotal* role to play in the positive outcomes for these cases.

However, in 13 of these 39 cases, all identified as being at high risk of re-offending and potentially dangerous (mainly convicted of violent and sex offences), the availability of social work services was a crucial element in the decision made. All of these cases were at their final review for parole purposes and the input of community based social work resources was considered essential as a means of risk management. Parole Board interviewees confirmed that these were the most difficult type of cases on which to make decisions. Where release on licence was recommended (in 11 of these cases), the Board's aim was to ensure that the prisoner would return to a controlled environment for a short period. The role of social work under these circumstances was less rehabilitative and more a means of keeping track of offenders.

Targeting resources and standards on the community based element of throughcare services is unlikely to encourage the Parole Board to release *greater* numbers of determinate sentence prisoners on licence at an *earlier* stage unless the Board changes its perspective on the context in which reduction in the risk of re-offending should take place. This would require the Board to accept that risk reduction should be effected in a community based rather than custodial setting.

Indeterminate Sentence Cases

For indeterminate sentence prisoners the principal focus of decision making was progress in custody. Key measures of progress were identified as: response to testing, for example on home leaves or in open conditions; and progress in addressing significant problems. The focus on change in custody meant that community based social work services did not feature in any of the decisions made in relation to this type of case.

A further impediment to policy impact may be the stage at which indeterminate sentence cases are referred to the Board. Release on licence for most cases will be at least one year away from the time at which the case is considered by the Board and dependent upon the successful completion of a pre-release programme. Detailed planning for release may not begin until the prisoner has been recommended for provisional release (as confirmed in a number of prison social work reports for indeterminate sentence cases in the report sample).

Impact of Prison Social Work Services on Decision making

The Board's focus on change during time spent in custody (both in respect of progress for indeterminate sentence cases and reduction in the level of risk of re-offending for determinate sentence cases) highlights the scope for high quality and effective prison based social work services to impact positively on parole decisions. However, Parole Board interviewees recognised that the impact of prison social work on the behaviour and attitudes of prisoners was often dependent on the motivation of the individual prisoner to change. Prisoners are not obliged to undertake counselling during time spent in custody and absence of motivation to change means that they will not generally be accepted on specialist programmes. In this respect, expansions in the range and quality of prison social work services may provide greater *opportunities* for prisoners to address their problems, but this will only impact on the Board's decision making practice where prisoners themselves choose to make use of these opportunities.

LIAISON

When asked about liaison Parole Board members had little to say. Liaison between the Parole Board and officials from SWSG and Scottish Prison Service (SPS) generally took place when officials attended the Parole Board's General Purposes meetings. While some were satisfied with these arrangements others felt that the Board required to be consulted more often about the development of policy.

CONCLUSION

Throughcare services were identified at Phase One of the research programme as being the most poorly developed element of social work criminal justice services. Interviewee responses indicate that the aspects of throughcare which impact on the parole process are still unevenly developed.

A key aim of Central Government is to facilitate common ownership of the policy in order that key criminal justice decision makers develop shared perspectives on, and have greater confidence in, the role of community based social work services in risk management. It would appear from the research findings of this study that common ownership does not as yet extend to the Parole Board.

CHAPTER ONE

SOCIAL WORK AND PAROLE

INTRODUCTION

In Scotland, statutory social work services to offenders and their families are provided by local authority social work departments. Since April 1991, The Scottish Office has reimbursed to social work departments the full costs of providing a range of statutory social work services in the criminal justice system. National Objectives and Standards (the National Standards) were introduced by the Social Work Services Group of The Scottish Office (SWSG) to coincide with the introduction of the funding initiative. The aim of the National Standards is to promote the development of high quality management and practice, the most efficient and effective use of resources and to provide social work services to the criminal justice system which have the confidence of both the courts and the wider public.

The National Standards and the funding initiative cover: social enquiry reports; court social work services; probation; community service[1] and certain specified elements of throughcare[2] (namely social work parole reports and the supervision of prisoners on release into the community). Since 1991, the initiative has been extended to supervised release orders, bail information and accommodation schemes, and supervised attendance orders (the latter two schemes are not available on a national basis). It is intended to include diversion from prosecution in the 100 per cent funding arrangements, subject to the progress of pilot schemes established in 1996. At present, fine supervision, means enquiry reports and deferred sentence supervision are not included in the funding initiative.

Prior to the introduction of the 100 per cent funding initiative and the National Standards, local authorities had to fund the majority of social work services out of their general income. Criminal justice services were, therefore, in competition for resources with other local authority services and as a result were not always of sufficient quantity and quality to meet the requirements of the court.

The aims of the Government's policy are[3]:

- to reduce the use of custody in the criminal justice system by increasing the availability, improving the quality and targeting the use of community based court disposals and throughcare services on those most at risk of custody, especially young adult repeat offenders;

- to enable offenders to address their offending behaviour and make a successful adjustment to law abiding life.

BACKGROUND TO THE RESEARCH

Central Government's review and evaluation of the implementation of the funding initiative and the National Standards involves a programme of inspection by the Social Work Services Inspectorate (SWSI), interpretation of statistics and a programme of research.

The research programme is being conducted in three phases. The main purpose of Phase One, which was undertaken in 1992-1993, was to examine the responses of key criminal justice decision makers and Scottish Office officials to the principal objectives of the policy and the early arrangements for its implementation (McAra, 1998). Phase Two (of which this study is a part) consists of five inter-related studies, conducted in 1994 - 1995, which examine progress towards policy objectives: the national and local context of policy implementation (Brown, Levy, and McIvor, 1998); sentencer decision making (Brown and Levy, 1998); Parole Board decision making (McAra, 1998a); the process and outcomes of probation (McIvor and Barry, 1998); and the process and outcomes of throughcare (McIvor and Barry, 1998a). Phase Three will look at the longer term impact of services for offenders.

Four sheriff court areas, each in separate social work authorities, were selected as study sites for Phase Two of the research programme to reflect areas of both high and low population density and to represent both

---

[1] The 100% funding initiative and National Objectives and Standards were first applied to community service in 1989.

[2] Throughcare is the provision of services to offenders in custody and on release.

[3] Evaluation Strategy Working Group, September 1990. More recent statements (the 1998 White Paper on Crime and Punishment, paragraphs 9.1 and 10.3) are consistent with these aims.

specialist and more generic forms of organising social work criminal justice services. The names of the four areas have been anonymised and are referred to as Scott, Wallace, Burns and Bruce.

THE IMPACT OF THE POLICY ON PAROLE BOARD DECISION MAKING

Background

- The system of parole for determinate sentence prisoners was established by the Criminal Justice Act 1967. The Parole Board for Scotland was set up in 1968 to advise the Secretary of State on:

- the release on licence and recall from licence of prisoners whose cases have been referred by the Secretary of State;

- the conditions of licences and the variation and change of such conditions.

Types of Case

The main types of case with which the Board deals are: determinate sentence prisoners referred for consideration of release on parole; indeterminate sentence cases referred for consideration of provisional release; and parole or life licencees referred for consideration of recall.

The procedures for parole changed as a result of the implementation of the Prisoners and Criminal Proceedings (Scotland) Act 1993. The new procedures apply to all prisoners serving sentences of four years or more who were sentenced on or after 1 October 1993. All the cases in the sample for this study were sentenced before that date and therefore were dealt with under the old arrangements[4]. (Detailed information about the procedures for parole and the key changes introduced by the Act are included in the report at Annex One.)

Parole Research

To date there has been little research undertaken on Parole Board decision making in Scotland and none specifically on the impact of social work services on the decision making process. Much research on parole in other jurisdictions has focused on the effectiveness of supervision of licencees and the development of risk prediction scales (Nuttall, 1997[5] and Ward, 1987[6].

Studies which have examined decision making in England and Wales have found that Parole Boards tend to be extremely cautious in their approach to decision making and that the decision making process is characterised by a high level of consensus amongst Board members (Morris and Beverly, 1975[7]; Hood and Shute, 1994[8]; Maguire, 1992[9].) Some commentators have argued that, in recent years, there has been a shift away from rehabilitative concerns in decision making towards a "justice model", with a corresponding emphasis on the rights of prisoners to equal treatment and consistency in decision making practice (Maguire, 1992). The most recent research on decision making in England and Wales (Hood and Shute, 1994) found that the main criteria used by Parole Boards in decisions to recommend parole, were good conduct in custody and good response to prison regimes. By contrast the criteria most frequently cited in decisions not to recommend release were the nature of the offence and criminal history, a key concern being risk to the public.

Social Work and Parole

Social workers have an important role to play in the parole process in Scotland, both in the provision of information to assist the Parole Board to make decisions in individual cases and in the supervision of parole and life licencees.

---

[4] A key element of Phase Two is to examine the impact of the wider policy context on policy implementation, including the impact of major criminal justice policies. This present study therefore includes an examination of Parole Board views on the potential impact of the Prisoners and Criminal Proceedings (Scotland) Act on its decision making practice.

[5] Nuttall, C.P. et. al (1977) *Parole in England and Wales,* HMSO.

[6] Ward, D. (1987) *The Validity of the Reconviction Prediction Score,* HMSO.

[7] Morris, P. and Beverly, F. (1975) *On Licence: A Study of Parole,* John Wiley.

[8] Hood, R. and Shute, S. (1994) *Parole in Transition. Evaluating the Impact and Effectiveness of Changes in the Parole System: Phase One,* Occasional Paper No. 13, Centre for Criminological Research Oxford.

[9] Maguire, M. in Stockdale, E. and Casale, S. eds. (1992) *Criminal Justice Under Stress,* Blackstone Press.

Information

The Parole Board is given a dossier for each prisoner which it considers for release on licence. The dossier comprises a number of reports, two of which are prepared by social workers: the prison social work report and the home circumstances report.

The prison social work report is prepared by a social worker in the establishment where the prisoner is currently serving their sentence. The report is intended to provide the Board with information about the prisoner's risk of re-offending and should also provide an opportunity for the discussion of release plans. The home circumstances report is prepared by a community based social worker from the area where the prisoner intends to reside on release. The main purpose of this report is to provide an assessment of the social and family context to which the prisoner is to return. It is also intended to contribute to the assessment of the risk of re-offending.

The National Standards set out detailed guidance on the preparation of these reports, including the key objectives of the reports and the types of information which they should cover. The evaluation of the impact of the policy on parole decision making therefore requires to examine the relationship between changes in the quality of these reports and the Parole Board's requirements for information in decision making.

Services

Social workers are responsible for the statutory supervision of prisoners released on parole or life licence. Community based social work supervision forms one element of throughcare services. These services are provided by social work and other associated agencies to prisoners and their families from the point of sentence or remand, during imprisonment and following release into the community. According to the National Standards, the principal objective of throughcare is to assist serving and released prisoners to address their offending behaviour and adjust to law abiding lives.

The National Standards and 100 per cent funding arrangements have been targeted on the community based element of throughcare. The evaluation therefore requires to examine the extent to which changes in the quality of community based social work services have been a key factor in the decisions which the Board take.

Prison based social work services do not come within the scope of the 100 per cent funding initiative nor are they, at the time of writing, subject to National Standards. A key issue identified at Phase One of the research was that social work criminal justice services which do not come within the scope of the 100 per cent funding initiative may be under-resourced and of low priority (McAra, 1998). An important element of Phase Two is to examine the relationship between social work services which come within the National Standards and the 100 per cent funding arrangements and those which do not. This present study therefore requires an examination of the impact of prison social work services on decision making.

Liaison

The National Standards state that the effectiveness of social work contributions to the criminal justice system can be enhanced through the development of liaison arrangements between social work and agencies working in the criminal justice system. An important aspect of the evaluation is to identify formal and informal liaison arrangements between agencies working within the parole process, including the Parole Board, and assess their contribution to decision making.

Study Aims and Objectives

The main objective of this study is to examine the impact of arrangements for implementing the policy on Parole Board decision making. The specific aims of the research are:

- to examine the relationship between home circumstance and prison based social work reports and parole decisions;

- to assess the extent to which changes in the quality of prison based social work services have made an impact on decision making;

- to consider the extent to which changes in the quality of statutory supervision of released prisoners has encouraged earlier release on licence;

- and to assess the impact of formal and informal liaison arrangements at local and Central Government level on Parole Board decision making.

Method

The research involved observation of the six Parole Board meetings held between January and March 1994. The observed meetings represent a quarter of the Board's annual business and in this respect the cases considered at the meetings reflect the range with which the Board deals. Transcripts (as near as possible verbatim) of the discussion at the six meetings were taken and the cases considered form the observation sample (n=311) in this study.

The observation transcripts enabled a detailed study to be undertaken of the factors which the Board takes into account when making decisions, and the extent to which these factors include services which prison and/or community based social work can offer.

To examine the relationship between information provided by social workers and parole decisions a sub-sample of cases considered at the observed meetings was drawn and the dossiers of these cases analysed (n=69, the report sample, see below).

As no base-line study was undertaken it was not possible to determine through the observational work nor the analysis of the dossiers, alone, whether any substantial changes in Parole Board decision making had occurred as a result of policy implementation. In order to examine this, semi-structured interviews were conducted with four out of the 14 members of the Parole Board for Scotland. The interviews explored Parole Board views on the quality of social work services (including both information and social work supervision) and the implications of the decision making patterns, identified during the observation, for policy implementation.

In order to obtain the social work perspective on the relationship between service quality and decision making, interviews were also undertaken with four prison social workers (one from each of the study prison units) in addition to four group interviews with community based social workers from each study site. More detailed information about the methods used is included in the report at Annex II.

Samples

Observation Sample

The main sample comprises all cases considered at the six observed meetings[10] as summarised in Table 1.1 These cases are representative of the range of case types on which the Board makes decisions. (During the observation period a number of these cases was referred to the Board on more than one occasion and therefore the number of decisions made on the observation sample totals 345.)

Table 1.1: Observation Sample

Type of Case	Number (n=311)
Determinate Sentence Cases	220
Indeterminate Sentence Cases	44
Cases referred for Consideration of Recall	47

Report Sample

The report sample comprises all cases discussed at the observed meetings from four prison units as summarised in Table 1.2. The prison units were selected from each study authority to reflect a range of units. These units cater for different categories of prisoner and the aim of the report sample was to cover the range of *case categories* (for example young adult offenders, lower and higher security classification prisoners) with which the Board deals. There are 69 cases in the report sample and these represent 26 per cent of the cases referred to the Board for *consideration of release* (n=264) during the observation[11].

---

[10] At these meetings the board also considered supervision reports on life licencees. Supervision reports do not form a part of the main sample cases. Although in principle decisions on these reports are the prerogative of the full Parole Board in practice the views of the member (who has responsibility for making recommendations on such reports) were rarely contested. It was therefore not possible to examine the decision making proces through observation.

[11] This excludes the 47 cases referred for consideration of recall.

Table 1.2: Report Sample

Study Site	Prison	Number Of Cases (n=69)
Burns	Closed Establishment. All Categories of Prisoner	4
Bruce	Closed Establishment. All Categories of Prisoner	30
Wallace	Open Establishment. Young Adult Male Offenders (aged 16 - 21)	8
Scott	Semi Open Establishment. Adult Male Prisoners with Security Category C or D	27

More detailed information about the samples is given in the report at Annex III.

Structure of the Report

Part One of the report examines: the quality of information provided by social workers to the Board; social work and Parole Board views on the impact of the policy on social work parole reports; and the impact of information on decision making.

Part Two examines Parole Board and social work views on: the quality of prison social work services; and whether policy implementation has led to any changes in range and quality of community based social work services. It also assesses the impact of social work services on Parole Board decision making in relation to cases referred for consideration of (provisional) release. This includes consideration of: determinate sentence cases in which factors relating to social work services were given as contributory reasons for decisions made, referred to as "impact cases"; determinate sentence cases where social work services did not feature in the reasons given by the Board for decisions made, referred to as "non-impact cases"; and indeterminate sentence cases.

Part Three explores Parole Board and social work views on the relationship between service quality and breach of licence and examines the decision making patterns in relation to cases referred for consideration of recall.

PART 1

INFORMATION AND DECISION MAKING

CHAPTER TWO

PRISON SOCIAL WORK REPORTS

INTRODUCTION

The National Standards state that the key purposes of prison social work reports are: to provide information which will assist the Parole Board to make decisions on the early release of determinate and indeterminate sentence prisoners; to identify and assess risk of further offending on release; and to provide an opportunity for the discussion of release plans[12].

This chapter assesses the quality of the information received by the Board from prison based social workers during the observation period, by measuring the prison social work reports from the Report Sample against the requirements of National Standards. It explores prison social work views on factors which impact on the quality of the reports which they provide and examines the relationship between the information requirements of the Parole Board and the National Standards for prison social work reports.

QUALITY OF INFORMATION: THE SAMPLE OF REPORTS

The sample of prison social work reports drawn for detailed analysis comprises all cases considered at the observed meetings, from each of the four study prison units[13].

Table 2.1: Sample of Prison Social Work Reports

Study Site	Prison	Number Of Reports (N=68)
Burns	Closed Establishment. All Categories of Prisoner	4
Bruce	Closed Establishment . All Categories of Prisoner	29*
Wallace	Open Establishment. Young Adult Male Offenders (aged 16 - 21)	8
Scott	Semi Open Establishment. Adult Male Prisoners with Security Category C or D	27

* Thirty cases were considered from the Bruce prison unit but one dossier did not include a prison social work report

Basis of Reports

The National Standards state that each prison social work report should be based on at least two interviews with the prisoner for the purposes of writing the report. In addition prison social workers must liaise with the social work department preparing the home circumstances report. Other supplementary sources of information are left to the discretion of the social worker although the Standards mention: the social worker's previous knowledge of the prisoner; and consultation with other prison based staff[14].

Of the reports in our sample only 16 (24 per cent) met National Standards in relation to the sources of information upon which the report was based. As Table 2.2 shows, reports were generally based on one interview with the prisoner only (27 or 40 per cent of reports), or at least two interviews with the prisoner but without any contact with community based social workers in the area to which the prisoner was returning (20 or 29 per cent of reports).

---

[12] Social Work Services Group (1991) *National Objectives and Standards for Social Work Services in the Criminal Justice System, Throughcare:* Paragraphs 35-37.

[13] As highlighted in Chapter One, the report sample was selected to cover the range of case categories with which the Board deals. It was *not* selected to be representative of prison social work reports in general.

[14] *National Objectives and Standards: Throughcare:* Paragraphs 40-42.

Table 2.2: Prison Social Work Reports: Basis

Basis	Percent (n=68)	
1 Interview with Prisoner	40	(27)
2+ Interviews with Prisoner	29	(20)
2 Interviews with Prisoner and Liaison with Community Social Worker	24	(16)
1 Interview with Prisoner and Liaison with Community Social Worker	3	(2)
Neither Interviews nor Liaison	4	(3)

Shaded area: reports meet National Standards
Numbers in brackets: actual number of reports

A high number of reports in the sample (62 or 91 per cent) had made use of sources of information other than interviews and contact with area teams. Most frequently mentioned additional sources (Table 2.3) were prison social work records and the social worker's own knowledge of the prisoner from previous contact. Other sources of information were: prison staff who had day to day contact with the prisoner; contact with the prisoner's family; agencies providing supported accommodation for prisoners with special needs; psychiatrists in one case where the prisoner had undergone psychiatric treatment during their sentence; and the social enquiry report.

Table 2.3: Prison Social Work Reports: Other Sources of Information

Source	Percent (n=68)	
Prison Social Work Records	60	(41)
Previous Contact	21	(14)
Prison Staff	13	(9)
Family Contact	12	(8)
Contact with Supported Accommodation Agency	4	(3)
Contact with Psychiatrist	1	(1)
Social Enquiry Report	1	(1)

Percentages add up to more than 100 because some reports were based on more than one source
Numbers in brackets: actual number of reports

Content of Reports

Prison social work reports are required by National Standards to *provide* and *assess* 11 types of information: the prisoner's personal circumstances; attitude towards the offence; attitude to sentence; attitude to release plans; response to imprisonment; employment prospects and use of leisure on release; substance misuse or gambling problems; response to previous supervision; family and other significant relationships; the availability of specialist resources in the community; and risk of re-offending.

As shown in Table 2.4, one of the reports in the sample *provided* all the types of information required by National Standards. Reports covered on average seven of the required areas with the best reports (as measured by the Standards) including ten types of information (four reports) and the poorest covering only two of the required areas (one report). All of the reports included a description of the prisoner's personal circumstances. Other areas which were well covered were: response to imprisonment; description of the offender's attitude towards their offence; employment prospects and use of leisure on release; and a description of the prisoner's family or other significant relationships. Areas less well covered were attitude towards the sentence and attitude towards release plans.

Table 2.4: Prison Social Work: Types of Information Provided

Type of Information	Percent (n=68)	
Personal Circumstances	100	(68)
Response to Imprisonment	94	(64)
Attitude towards the Offence	90	(61)
Employment Prospects or Use of Leisure	87	(59)
Family or Other Significant Relationships	85	(58)
Substance Misuse or Gambling Problems	82	(56)
Response to Previous Supervision	53	(36)
Risk of Re-offending	51	(35)
Services Available in the Community	50	(34)
Attitude towards Sentence	38	(26)
Attitude towards Release Plans	12	(8)

Percentages add up to more than 100 as reports included more than one type of information
Numbers in brackets: actual number of reports

Overall, the reports in the sample tended to be descriptive rather than analytical. For example, while the prison social worker might describe the membership of the prisoner's family in the report they often did not provide an assessment of the relationships (85 per cent of reports included a description of family relationships but only 26 per cent of reports assessed the quality of relationships). Similarly while a high number of reports made mention of the prisoner's own views on the extent to which their drug or alcohol problems had been addressed (82 per cent of reports), substantially fewer gave the social worker's assessment of their progress (46 per cent of reports). To use the terms given in the National Standards, the reports in the sample were better at "indicating" problems than assessing the extent of them.

In the sample of reports, out of a total of 11 assessments required by National Standards, reports on average included four, with the best report in the sample including eight assessments and three reports making no assessments. As indicated in Table 2.5, most reports included an assessment of the personal circumstances of the prisoner, in particular their domestic circumstances and accommodation on release; the prisoner's response to imprisonment, and their attitude to the offence. Areas which were less well covered were attitude to release plans, attitude to sentence, and family and other relationships. Around half of the reports in the sample (35) included an assessment of risk of re-offending.

Table 2.5: Prison Social Work Reports: Assessments Made

Assessment	Percent (n=68)	
Personal Circumstances	72	(49)
Response to Imprisonment	66	(45)
Attitude towards the Offence	59	(40)
Risk of Re-offending	51	(35)
Services Available on Release. (Mentioned as part of an assessment of need)	50	(34)
Response to Previous Supervision	46	(31)
Substance Misuse or Gambling Problems	46	(31)
Employment Prospects or Use of Leisure	34	(23)
Family or Other Significant Relationships	26	(18)
Attitude towards Sentence	24	(16)
Attitude Towards Release Plans	10	(7)

Percentages add up to more than 100 as most reports included more than one type of assessment
Numbers in brackets: actual number of reports

Risk Assessments

As highlighted above, one of the principal objectives of the prison social work report is to identify and assess risk of further offending on release. The supplement to the National Standards[15] highlights a number of factors which are indicators of an increased risk of re-offending. These can be categorised into three main types: criminal history[16]; personal characteristics in respect of age and sex[17]; and the range and intensity of social, family and personal problems experienced by the individual and which are associated with criminal behaviour.

The 35 reports in the sample which included a risk assessment used a narrower range of indicators than those suggested in the National Standards. Most risk assessments focused on the extent to which the prisoner had addressed their offending behaviour during time spent in custody (17 or 49 per cent of reports which included a risk assessment); whether the prisoner had overcome any addiction problems (9 or 26 per cent) ; if the offence had been "out of character", thereby assessing the link between the prisoner's previous lifestyle and their offending (8 or 23 per cent); and whether the deterrent effect of the sentence had been met (5 or 14 per cent).

REPORT PREPARATION: SOCIAL WORK VIEWS ON QUALITY

Prison social work interviewees were asked to comment on their approach to report writing and the extent to which National Standards implementation had led to improvements in the quality of reports which they prepared.

Time-scale

Interviewees commented that they usually were given around six weeks notice in which to prepare prison social work reports. Most considered that it was easy to deliver reports on time. However, one interviewee commented that increased workloads (which had occurred because of a change that had recently been made to the function of their prison unit) made it difficult to meet deadlines.

Basis of Reports

Although only 27 per cent of reports in the sample showed evidence of contact with area teams, the majority (3) of prison social work interviewees stated that they always made contact with the social work department in the area to which the prisoner would be returning. They noted that arrangements for contacting area teams generally worked well. However, two of these three interviewees commented that it was sometimes difficult to find out which social worker was preparing the home circumstances report because of delays in appointing a supervising officer for a case.

A majority of interviewees reported that the level of contact with area teams had increased since National Standards implementation. Previously they had only contacted area teams when a prisoner had special needs, for example where supported accommodation or residential drug treatment would be required on release. Now contact was made on a routine basis. One interviewee, however, did not consider that contact with community social workers was always necessary. It was their practice to liaise only where there were "significant issues" which required to be resolved. This interviewee also reported that they rarely conducted more than one interview with the prisoner for the purposes of preparing the parole report. They believed that all the necessary information could be obtained at one interview and workloads made second interviews difficult to arrange.

Making Assessments

Interviewee responses indicate that some types of assessment may be easier for social workers to make than other types. Assessments of response to imprisonment, substance misuse and gambling problems were believed to be easier to make when the prisoner had had direct contact with the prison social work unit or other specialist agencies during the course of their sentence. However, prisoners are not obliged to make use of services which social work provides[18]. A number of prison social work interviewees commented that although

---

15 *National Objectives and Standards: Social Work Supervision:* Towards Effective Policy and Practice.

16 This includes: number of previous convictions; age when first dealt with by the courts or the children's hearings for criminal matters; length of time between previous and current conviction; number of associates in current offence.

17 According to the supplement to the National Standards: the younger the person is, the more likely they are to re-offend; and male offenders are more likely to re-offend than female offenders.

18 Scottish Prison Service policy (SPS, (1990), *Opportunity and Responsibility,* HMSO) states that prisoners should not be regarded as persons in need of treatment but as responsible people who should be provided with a range of services which they can choose to make use of during their sentence.

parole eligible prisoners were treated as a priority group for services, sometimes the only contact which they had with a prisoner was at the first interview for the purposes of preparing the parole report.

Assessments of family and other significant relationships and domestic arrangements (which is included in the personal circumstances assessment) were reported as being difficult to make on occasions. The accuracy of assessments was felt to be dependent on the quality of information which could be provided by area teams and this, in turn, was considered to depend on how well social workers in the area knew the prisoner's family. Much of the available information which prison social workers had to base assessments on was described as "subjective". Two interviewees commented that they often had to rely on the prisoner's own account of the level of family support or the suitability of domestic arrangements as workloads did not permit them to verify information. This was not however considered to be problematic as, in their view, other reports in the dossier would either confirm the information given by the prisoner or refute it[19].

> "I have to base my reports solely on my assessment of the prisoner's response to questions. ..People do tend to be honest and if they're not there would be information elsewhere in the dossier which would make it obvious. If I had loads of time I could check out information." (Prison Social Worker)

One prison social work interviewee considered that providing an assessment of family or other significant relationships should not be their responsibility. The author of the home circumstances report was felt to be better placed to make these assessments.

There were variations of view about the ease of making assessments of the prisoner's response to previous social work supervision. The key source of information for such assessments was social work department records. A number of interviewees had experienced difficulties in the past in accessing records. This was attributed to the competence of individual social work departments in record keeping. Other interviewees by contrast reported that they never had any difficulties in accessing the relevant records. There was consensus amongst interviewees however that access to records was only sought once the prisoner's permission had been given. If permission was not given, then assessments on response to previous supervision would be more difficult to make.

A common view amongst prison social work interviewees was that assessments of risk of re-offending were also extremely difficult to make. As with other assessments, difficulties were linked to lack of relevant information. Most interviewees agreed that they were often "working in the dark" as they did not generally have access to verified information about the index offence or previous convictions. (In this respect social workers did not have sufficient information to enable them to assess risk according to the guidance in the National Standards highlighted above.) Some social workers reported that they had access to prison files but these were considered to be superficial. Only in one of the prison units was the note of circumstance[20] regularly available. As a result of limited information, social workers often had to rely on the prisoner for details of the offence and this was viewed as being highly problematic.

> "There's no verified information and that's dangerous. A lifer I worked with said he had just hit someone over the head with a bottle but [I found out later] he also stabbed him eight times with a kitchen knife, strangled him with a leather belt and hit him over the head with a kitchen clock - a frenzied attack...that gave me a different insight. [We are] unable to get the information to get that insight easily." (Prison Social Worker)

A further difficulty in making risk assessments related to the criteria used to measure risk. Interviewees commented that it was often "impossible" to predict future behaviour, particularly in relation to substance misuse. Although a prisoner might have made some progress in addressing their addiction problems within a prison based setting it was difficult to assess what their reaction would be on release when such substances were more readily available. Similarly any change in the prisoner's attitude to the offence was difficult to measure without access to verified information on the offence.

Social Workers found it particularly difficult to make risk assessments of indeterminate sentence prisoners. This was because such prisoners were often first offenders with no history of violent behaviour:

> "Lifers are an area I find very difficult...you're talking about a one-off offence. The majority of lifers did not intend to kill their victims so the consequences of their actions are greater. In one of my groups there's one doing four years for attempted murder. Now he had stabbed his victim 27 times. A lifer in the group who disarmed his victim stabbed him once.......They can have a totally unblemished prison career but to me that's not an indicator. Its an area no one finds easy. I don't always offer a risk assessment because I wouldn't feel equipped to do it." (Prison Social Worker)

---

[19] One of these interviewees had commented earlier, however, that they found it easy to prepare reports on time. It would appear that this interviewee adopted a pragmatic approach to report writing. Where information would be included in other reports in the dossier and where there was limited time to verify information, then this social worker would, as a matter of routine, include information without verification in order to meet report deadlines. In this respect by not checking out information with other sources, reports were easy to deliver on time.

[20] The note of circumstance is prepared by The Scottish Office Home Department. It gives details of the nature and circumstances of the offence.

These comments are borne out by the analysis of the sample of prison social work reports. Most of the reports where no assessment was offered were for indeterminate sentence prisoners (24 or 73 per cent of reports which did not include a risk assessment).

Developing a Release Package

As highlighted above, only half of the reports in the sample indicated services in the community which might be available to minimise the risks of re-offending and assist the prisoner to re-integrate into the community. Interviewees were asked about the circumstances under which they would provide a release package for a prisoner.

A common perception amongst interviewees was that the development of a potential release plan was primarily the responsibility of the social worker preparing the home circumstances report. As a consequence they seldom included such a plan in their reports.

> "The area team should identify resources. It's not of paramount importance in my reports." (Social Worker)

> "It's not my role to provide a release package. My stuff is really risk of offending, but I suppose I would check out the availability of services. If I make a recommendation I always check out services." (Social Worker)

Cases for which these social workers generally drew up a provisional release plan were where the prisoner had undertaken counselling in prison to deal with significant problems and follow-up counselling in the community was considered to be of benefit; or where the prisoner had special needs, for example prisoners with behavioural problems who required supported accommodation.

A further interviewee commented that while they recognised the importance of providing provisional release plans, they would not develop a plan unless, in their view, it was likely that the prisoner would be recommended for parole.

There was consensus amongst prison social work interviewees that the development of a release package was dependent on both the knowledge which individual social workers had about the prisoner and the level of information which they had about services which were available in the community to which the prisoner would be returning. As highlighted above, the parole interview was sometimes the first contact which the social work unit had with a prisoner. Under these circumstances, unless high quality information on the prisoner was available from other sources, it was extremely difficult for social workers to assess and plan for the prisoner's individual needs.

Interviewees agreed that the author of the home circumstances report was a key source of information on the suitability and availability of community based services. However, on the occasions where liaison between prison social workers and community based social workers did not operate well, identification of suitable services was described as a "bit of a hit or miss affair". Most interviewees commented that they had gradually built up their own directory of services: one suggested that it would be helpful if a national directory was drawn up but recognised that this would be resource intensive.

Impact of National Standards on Report Writing

Most prison social workers interviewed agreed that National Standards had impacted positively on their report writing. The Standards provided clear guidelines for reports and social workers reported that they now focused more on the offence and offending behaviour. None of the interviewees had received specific training in writing parole reports although a number had undertaken social enquiry report training and this was considered to have been helpful.

One interviewee commented, however, that changes that they had made in their approach to report writing had occurred not because of Standards implementation but because of feedback on cases for which they had prepared reports. Formerly this social worker had included prisoners' accounts of the offence in their reports. In a number of cases the Board had, in their view, misinterpreted the accounts as indicating that the prisoner had not addressed their offending behaviour and consequently remained a high risk case. Now when this interviewee prepared reports, they did not include details of the offence but only provided an assessment of the prisoner's attitude.

To summarise, prison social work interviewee responses provide a number of explanations as to why the prison social work reports in the sample did not always meet Standards requirements. The relatively poor coverage of a number of key assessments in reports may be attributable to inadequacies in the information available to social workers, especially in relation to criminal history and verified information on the nature of the offence.

Workloads too may have limited social workers' ability to put the Standards into practice. The small number of reports which included a release package may also be a reflection of the views of some prison social workers that the preparation of a release package should be the responsibility of the author of the home circumstances report.

PAROLE BOARD VIEWS ON REPORTS

Parole Board interviewees were asked about the information they expected to receive from prison social work reports, and for their views on: the quality of prison social work reports; the extent to which they had noticed any changes in quality since National Standards implementation; and the impact of reports on the decisions which they made.

Expectations of Prison Social Work Reports

There was consensus amongst Parole Board interviewees that the key purpose of the prison social work report should be to provide information about the prisoner's plans for release; their progress in custody and the extent to which they had addressed any significant problems, in particular whether the prisoner had addressed addiction problems or other behaviour associated with offending. The report was identified as a key source of information on the level of risk which a prisoner posed. These views are confirmed in part by the decision making patterns of the Board during the observation period. When reference was made in presentations and discussions of cases to prison social work reports, this was most frequently in relation to the social worker's assessment of risk and the extent to which the prisoner had addressed their offending behaviour[21].

Interviewee responses indicate that there is a high level of correspondence between the Board's expectation of prison social work reports and the type of information required by National Standards. The reports in the sample would suggest, however, that the Board does not always receive reports which meet its requirements. As highlighted above, while over half of the reports did include assessments of response to custody (66 per cent) and the offender's attitude towards the offence (59 per cent), only one half of the reports included a risk assessment, and less than half included an assessment of addiction problems and the prisoner's attitude towards their release plans.

Views on Quality

If the reports in the sample were typical of those generally submitted to the Parole Board, it could be expected that Parole Board interviewees might express dissatisfaction with the quality of prison social work reports. However the majority (3) of interviewees were generally satisfied with the reports that they received. One of these three interviewees did not know what the contents of the Standards were and was therefore not in a position to comment on the relationship between the quality of reports and National Standards. The other two of these interviewees generally attributed quality both to National Standards implementation and also to the greater specialisation of social workers in offender services in recent years. National Standards implementation was considered in particular to have led to better structured reports.

> "They're more confident than they used to be, they're clearer and not defensive. They try to evidence things more. The quality of reports can be dependent on the opportunities which the social worker has to get to know the prisoner. National Standards mean that where social workers don't get the opportunity they have a checklist and this makes for better reports."(Parole Board Member)

When asked to comment on the apparent contradiction between expressions of satisfaction with the reports and the poor quality of some of the information in the report sample, interviewees stated that the prison social work reports in the sample could not be typical of the reports which they usually received.

As highlighted in Chapter One, the sample of prison social work reports was selected to cover a range of case categories from prison units in the study sites. It was not selected to be representative of all prison social work reports. The responses of these interviewees could therefore be taken to indicate that the general quality of

---

[21] Reference was made to prison social work reports in 87 (30%) out of 290 "relevant" decisions. (Only 290 of the 345 observed decisions are relevant. The remaining 55 decisions related to recall cases for which the Board had neither prison social work nor home circumstances reports.) This cannot be taken to imply however that information provided by prison social work reports was not important in the remainder of the "relevant" decisions. Board members sometimes did not indicate the source of information which formed the focus of their presentations and/or discussions. Of the 87 decisions in which reference was made to the prison social work report, risk assessments were referred to in 24 (28%) of decisions. Other information referred to was as follows: social work recommendation on outcome (not a requirement of National Standards) 15 (17%) of decisions; alcohol problems 9 (10%); drug problems 9 (10%); relationship counselling undertaken 6 (5%); home circumstances 4 (5%); mental health problems 4 (5%); recommendation for additional requirements in licence/services to meet needs 4 (5%); release plans (unspecified) 3 (3%); anger control problems 2 (2%); employment prospects 1 (1%); debt 1 (1%); and sex offender counselling 1(1%).

prison social work reports (as measured by the National Standards) is higher than the quality of some of the reports in the sample. However, this conclusion is not borne out by the views of the fourth Parole Board interviewee who expressed dissatisfaction with prison social work reports. In the view of this Board member, reports often lacked clarity and did not include all the types of information for which they looked, in particular: assessments of the extent to which a prisoner had addressed their offending; details of counselling which the prisoner had undertaken in prison; and an assessment of the prisoner's release plans.

> "A third are good, a third are not good and a third are terrible. Sometimes they put things in that don't resemble anything else in the dossier. When reports meet the Standards they stand out a mile." (Parole Board Member)

This interviewee linked the quality of what, in their view, were good reports less to National Standards and more to the experience of the individual social worker.

During the observation period the quality of prison social work reports was rarely an explicit factor in decision-making. Comments on quality were only made in 17 (6 per cent) out of 290 relevant decisions. In three of these decisions the quality of the prison social work report was singled out for praise, mainly in respect of the social worker's assessment of the prisoner's progress and efforts to develop a suitable release plan. However, in the other 14 decisions the Board made reference to the poor quality of the report. This was mainly where reports had failed to include information on the prisoner's previous response to social work supervision and/or efforts to address offending behaviour (10 decisions), or where the reports did not indicate the prisoner's plans for release (4 decisions). Importantly, however, the poor quality of information had a direct impact on the outcome of only three cases which were deferred in order that the prison social worker could have more time to provide the required information. In the other 11 decisions the poor quality of the prison social work reports did not impact directly on outcomes as there were other features of the cases which the Board considered to be more significant[22].

Views on Impact of Reports on Decision making

There was consensus amongst Parole Board interviewees that when making decisions on individual cases they took into account the range of reports in the parole dossier and that this would limit the impact which an individual report could have. For example, while the prison social work report was cited as an important source of information on risk, it was the practice of the Board to compare and contrast the assessments made in the prison social work report with the prisoner's own account of the offence, as outlined in their representations, and with official accounts of the offence provided in the note of circumstance or police report. In this respect the prison social work report was one piece of evidence to be weighed up against other information in the dossier.

> "I look for correlations between reports or disagreements which don't match. I'd look at the note of circumstance to get some indication of the offence and what was involved and see how that matches up with what other people's assessments are based on and what the prisoner is telling me. How close is his account, how much dodging of detail." (Parole Board Member)

SUMMARY

The prison social work reports in the sample suggest that the Parole Board does not always receive reports which meet its requirements for information, a key feature being the lack of assessments of risk of re-offending and the extent to which prisoners had addressed their substance misuse problems. However, most Parole Board interviewees were generally satisfied with the reports which they received, and suggested that the reports in the sample may not be typical of the general quality of prison social work reports. These interviewees attributed improved quality of reports to National Standards implementation. Only one interviewee considered that the general quality of reports was poor and that National Standards had made minimal impact.

Social work interviewee responses indicate that the quality of information provided in prison social work reports is dependent upon the social worker's own knowledge of the prisoner (which in turn is dependent primarily on the prisoner choosing to make use of social work services in prison during their sentence), ease of access to relevant information, and good liaison with community based social workers.

---

[22] In five cases a negative outcome was given as the prisoner was considered to be at too high a risk of re-offending or had made insufficient progress to warrant parole; in six cases a release or a forward release date was recommended as other information in the dossier indicated a number of positive aspects of the case.

Although social workers considered that they had changed their approach to report writing since National Standards implementation, the workload of some interviewees would appear to have limited the extent to which they could put the Standards into practice. Workloads were identified as limiting, in particular, the time available for social workers to verify information and the number of interviews which social workers were able to conduct with the prisoner for the purpose of preparing the report. Importantly some prison social work interviewees considered that certain elements of reports, required by National Standards, should not be the primary responsibility of the prison social worker, in particular assessments of family and other significant relationships, and the development of release plans. These views account in part for the low number of such assessments and release plans included in the sample of reports.

CHAPTER THREE

HOME CIRCUMSTANCES REPORTS

INTRODUCTION

The National Standards state that home circumstances reports should: describe and assess the social and family context to which the prisoner intends to return; indicate the nature of supervision which will be provided and any specialist facilities which might be offered; contribute to the assessment of risk of re-offending; and engage the prisoner's family in planning for the prisoner's release.

This chapter assesses the quality of information provided to the Parole Board by community based social workers, by measuring the sample of home circumstances reports against the requirements of the National Standards. It explores the views of community based social workers on factors impacting on the quality of reports and examines the relationship between the Board's requirements for information and the guidance provided by the National Standards on the preparation of home circumstances reports.

QUALITY OF INFORMATION: THE SAMPLE OF REPORTS

The sample of home circumstances reports was drawn from the same parole dossiers as the sample of prison social work reports considered in Chapter Two. The sample comprises 63 reports as six of the parole dossiers did not include a home circumstances report. Prisoners associated with the sample reports were being considered for release to a wide range of areas (including the study sites) within Scotland and, coincidentally, none of the reports were prepared by the community social workers interviewed from each study site.

Basis of Reports

The Standards state that home circumstances reports should be based on at least one home visit to, and one interview with the prisoner's family or other persons with whom the prisoner intends to live (all of the prisoners associated with the home circumstances reports in the sample had families to which they were to return) and contact and liaison with the relevant prison social worker.

Of the 63 reports in our sample only 12 (19 per cent) reports met National Standards in this respect. Most reports were based on one interview with the family and gave no evidence that the prison social worker had been contacted (Table 3.1).

Table 3.1: Home Circumstances Reports: Basis

Basis of Report	Percent (n=63)	
Family Only*	65	(41)
Prison Social Worker Only	2	(1)
Both	19	(12)
Contact with Neither Family nor Prison Social Worker	16	(10)

*Prisoner's family or other persons with whom they intend to live
  Shaded area: reports meet Standards
  Percentages add up to more than 100 because of rounding
  Numbers in brackets: actual number of reports

Most home circumstances reports in the sample indicated that the author had consulted other sources of information when preparing the report. In 11 (17 per cent) reports the social worker stated that they had previous knowledge of the prisoner and that they were able to draw on this to make assessments. Other sources mentioned were: departmental files (16 or 25 per cent of reports); interviews with the prisoner (15 or 24 per cent of reports) and, in a few cases, the social enquiry report (4 or 6 per cent of reports).

Types of Information

According to National Standards, home circumstances reports should provide and assess six main types of information: background information, including housing and financial factors; family attitude towards the prisoner; the environment to which the prisoner is to return; specialist programmes or resources in the community; the family's likely response to social work supervision of the prisoner (or the attitude of other persons with whom the prisoner intends to live); as well as an overview of: risk factors in relation to re-offending, social or personal breakdown; support; and particular needs.

Reports in the sample included on average four of the required six types of information. Ten (16 per cent) reports in the sample included all six types with one report including only one of the required types of information. Types of information which were well covered in reports (Table 3.2) were background information, especially in relation to accommodation, and family attitudes towards the prisoner and the environment to which the prisoner was to return. Less well covered types of information were specialist resources available on release, and family attitude towards social work supervision .

Although a high proportion of reports (46 or 73 per cent of reports) included an overall indication of either risk factors or support or needs, only ten reports (16 per cent) included all three.

Table 3.2: Home Circumstances Reports: Types of Information Provided

Type Of Information	Percent (n=63)	
Background	94	(59)
Family Attitudes	90	(57)
Environment	75	(47)
Specialist Resources	48	(30)
Family Attitude to SW Supervision	43	(27)
Overall assessment Support, Risk, Need	73	(46)
Support	73	(46)
Risk	40	(25)
Need	32	(20)

Percentages add up to more than 100 as reports included more than one type of information.
Numbers in brackets: actual number of reports

Assessments

The home circumstances reports in the sample tended to be descriptive rather than analytical. For example although a high number of reports included a description of household members' attitudes towards the prisoner's return (57 or 90 per cent of reports), rather fewer included the social worker's own assessment of this (24 or 38 per cent) as seen in Table 3.3. Reports on average gave an assessment of only two out of the six types of information which required to be assessed. Three reports (5 per cent) included assessments of all six types of information but ten reports (15 per cent) gave no assessments at all. The most frequent assessments given were in relation to background information on housing and domestic arrangements (48 or 76 per cent of reports) and overall level of support (46 or 73 per cent) with fewer than half of the reports including assessments of other areas.

Table 3.3: Home Circumstances Reports: Assessments Made

Assessment	Percent (n=63)	
Background	76	(48)
Suitability of Specialist Resources	46	(29)
Environment	46	(29)
Family Attitude	38	(24)
Overall Assessment		
Support	73	(46)
Risk	40	(25)
Needs	32	(20)
Family Attitude to Supervision	10	(6)

Percentages add up to more than 100 because reports included much more than one type of assessment
Numbers in brackets: actual number of reports

As highlighted in the introduction to this chapter, one of the main objectives of the home circumstances reports is to contribute to the assessment of risk of re-offending. Of the 25 home circumstances reports in the sample which included an overall assessment of risk, most focused the assessment on the level of family support which the prisoner would have on release (Table 3.4). Other less frequently mentioned factors were: the level of addiction problems and whether drugs were readily available in the community to which the offender would return; the extent to which the prisoner's associates in the community were involved in crime; whether the offender had addressed their offending behaviour; and employment opportunities.

Table 3.4 Home Circumstances Reports: Risk Assessments

Risk Indicator	Percent (n=25)	
Support	88	(22)
Substance Misuse	28	(7)
Associates in the Community	20	(5)
Addressing Offending	12	(3)
Employment Opportunities	8	(2)

Percentages add up to more than 100 because most reports included more than one indicator
Numbers in brackets: actual number of reports

As with prison social work reports, it would appear that the authors of home circumstances reports use fewer indicators than those included in the National Standards guidance, with most of the indicators relating to the likely impact of future plans and social circumstances on the offender's behaviour or the extent of change during custody.

COMMUNITY BASED SOCIAL WORK VIEWS ON REPORTS

Most community based social workers agreed that the key purpose of the home circumstances report was to provide information on domestic circumstances, family relationships, employment prospects and the response of the wider community to the prisoner's return. However, some community based social workers commented that the key purpose of the report was to provide information about the suitability of the release address only, a view which diverges from the objectives of the home circumstances reports as set out in the National Standards.

> "I gave very basic information. What they really want to know is if the release address is OK. The report has no other value." (Community based Social Worker)

In one area (Scott) social workers commented that their line managers had given them instructions to provide only this type of information.

Time-scale

Social work interviewees commented that usually they were given around six weeks notice for the preparation of home circumstances reports. In three areas (Bruce, Wallace and Scott) social workers considered that they had ample time for report preparation. However in one area (Burns) social enquiry reports were given higher priority and a number of social workers there said that delays in preparing home circumstances reports might occur during periods when a large number of social enquiry reports were required by the courts.

Basis of Report

Most interviewees commented that they always made contact with the prison social worker for the purposes of preparing the home circumstances report. While arrangements generally worked well, some interviewees reported that where a prison social work unit was staffed by a singleton worker, it was sometimes difficult to make contact with them.

Assessments

The ease of making assessments was directly linked to the type of information to which the social worker had access and to the level of cooperation received from professionals in other agencies.

All community based social work interviewees agreed that factors relating to risk of re-offending were extremely difficult to assess as they too lacked information about the prisoner's index offence and previous convictions. Social workers said that they might contact the prison social worker for information relating to the offence but they recognised that prison social workers often did not have access to the relevant information either. One social worker said that they had on occasions contacted the procurator fiscal for details of the charge and if this was unavailable they would make use of the local library newspaper archives for information.

It was easier for social workers to make assessments if they had access to, or, in a minority of cases, had been the author of the prisoner's social enquiry report. However, as there was no guarantee that prisoners would be returning to the same area where the social enquiry report had been prepared, access to these reports was limited.

A common view was that a proper assessment of risk could only be undertaken if the social worker had direct contact with the prisoner to discuss the offence and their attitude to their offending behaviour.

The difficulties in obtaining relevant information meant that some social workers were unable to provide a risk assessment in every report which they prepared. A number of interviewees went so far as to comment that it was inappropriate to provide such an assessment within the context of a home circumstances report:

> "I generally don't see this as my job. The key focus of my report is what happens when the offender comes back" (Community based Social Worker)

> "It's important that it's included in the dossier - but it's not appropriate for us to do it, given the limited facts that we can take into account. The prison social worker is best placed." (Community based Social Worker)

In contrast to assessments of risk, interviewees considered that it was relatively easy to make assessments of: family attitude to supervision; overall level of support; the environment to which the prisoner was to return; and background information, for example on housing or financial matters. This was because they had direct contact with the prisoner's family through interview and local knowledge of the area. However, assessments of the prisoner's needs and ways of meeting them were considered to be more difficult to make where the social worker had no prior knowledge of the prisoner.

> "It's not a problem if they're people you know. But if you have to start from scratch it's very difficult, you need time. If it's a person you've never met, do you have the right to go ahead and make plans on their behalf?" (Community based Social Worker)

Some interviewees had in the past visited the prisoner but it was recognised that this was not practicable in all cases, given the nature of their workloads and the distances sometimes involved. Furthermore, social work managers in one area (Scott) would not sanction such visits because of limited resources.

Undertaking a needs assessment was considerably eased where the prison social worker had already completed their report when contacted by the author of the home circumstances report. In such cases social workers were able to make use of the prison social worker's assessment as a basis for this element of their report. Good co-ordination between the prison social worker and the community social worker over the timing of report preparation was considered to be crucial. In practice, however, co-ordination was sometimes difficult to achieve.

> "It's unusual for me to phone the prison social worker to find out they're ahead of me in preparing the reports. Generally they'll say 'we're waiting for you to learn what your report says before we interview'. But that means that if you visit the prisoner's home address you don't have any information about the prisoner and the prison social worker's not met them either and therefore that delays you." (Social Worker)

A number of social work interviewees commented that there were several overlapping areas in prison social work and home circumstances reports and that it was often a "grey area" as to which social workers should take lead responsibility for retrieving relevant information and for providing assessments. A key issue was which social worker should develop a release package for the prisoner and set up the required services. There was an expectation amongst several community based social work interviewees that this would be undertaken by the prison social worker. This was because of their view (highlighted above) that the primary purpose of the home circumstances report was to provide information about the suitability of the release address.

Specialist Resources

While most social workers agreed that it was easy to give an indication of the types of specialist programmes available in the community to which the prisoner was to return it was sometimes difficult to refer cases to specialist agencies at the time of report preparation. For example, in one area social workers reported that they had difficulties in referring cases to supported accommodation agencies. Such agencies were often over-subscribed and would not guarantee a place for the prisoner unless the social worker could guarantee in turn that the prisoner would definitely be granted parole. When a prisoner was recommended for an early review[23] by the Parole Board rather than release on parole, the placement could fall through.

Offenders with mental health problems were identified by a number of interviewees as a key group for which it was difficult to make referrals to specialist programmes at the report writing stage. A common experience was the difficulty in obtaining a community care assessment for such prisoners, as community care teams did not consider that offenders fell within their remit. In one area (Bruce) the practice team manager required to negotiate with the community care team managers over individual cases.

Feedback on Quality of Reports and Outcomes

Most social workers reported that they never had any feedback on reports which they prepared for the Parole Board. In one study site (Scott) social workers said that middle managers in the social work department occasionally received information about the quality of individual reports and this would be passed on to the social worker who had prepared the report. Most agreed that if they had a clearer understanding of Parole Board expectations, this would improve the quality of the reports which they wrote.

> "More feedback would be helpful. Not face to face, but to indicate how our reports are received, the level of detail required, are we addressing the right areas. If the Board has considered a case a couple of times before and there is a particular area they want us to look at we've no way of knowing. It's like sending reports into a black hole." (Community based Social Worker)

A key concern was that social workers rarely received information about the outcome of a case. While the National Standards state that the author of the home circumstances report should inform the family of the prisoner about the outcome of the parole decision, a number of interviewees commented that they often found out about the outcome from the families.

> "It would be nice to get the outcome. Families get informed before we do, from the prisoner. We're supposed to give the family the information but they tell us." (Community based Social Worker).

Social workers attributed lack of information to failures on the part of The Scottish Office Home Department to provide timeous feedback to local authority social work departments on the outcome of individual cases.

Impact of National Standards on Report Writing

A number of social workers interviewed commented that they were inexperienced at writing home circumstances reports (most had to prepare only one or two reports per year) and that they found that National Standards were helpful as a checklist. All agreed that they had changed their approach to report writing since National Standards implementation. Reports were now believed to be better structured and more focused. However, as with prison social workers interviewed, none of the community based social workers had undertaken specific training in parole report writing, although most had undertaken social enquiry report training.

PAROLE BOARD VIEWS ON REPORTS

Parole Board interviewees were asked about the information which they expected to receive from home circumstances reports and for their views on the quality of reports, the extent to which they had noticed any changes in the quality since National Standards implementation, and the impact of reports on the decisions which they made.

Expectations of Reports

Parole Board interviewees commented that the key purpose of the home circumstances report should be to provide information on: the suitability of the release address; an assessment of family relationships and the family's likely response to supervision of the prisoner; information about the prisoner's release plans, including services and supervision which social work could offer to meet the prisoner's needs. The home circumstances report was also perceived to be a key source of information on risk of re-offending. In these respects there is a high level of correspondence between the Parole Board's requirements for information and the guidance provided in the National Standards in respect of report preparation.

However, from the decisions made by the Parole Board during the observation period, it would appear that, in practice, the Board uses the home circumstances report mainly for information on the level of family support

---

[23] An early review is where the prisoner is not recommended for release on parole at current review but where the Board agree to review the case before the normal date at which the case would be re-referred for consideration of release (one year).

which the prisoner would receive[24]. This is one element of the home circumstances report which was generally well covered in the reports in the sample.

Views on Quality

There were variations of view about the quality of home circumstances reports in general and the impact of the National Standards in particular. Most interviewees considered that the overall standard of reports was lower than prison social work reports.

Two interviewees expressed concern that home circumstances reports were often cursory, giving little indication that they were based on verified sources of information or that there had been any collaboration between the author of the report and the prison social worker. These interviewees also reported that home circumstances reports were frequently missing from parole dossiers. Sometimes a letter from a specialist agency, confirming a placement, was provided as a substitute for a report. This was felt to be unsatisfactory, as social workers were responsible for overseeing the supervision of the prisoner on release in the community. Parole Board members who shared these views did not consider that National Standards implementation had impacted on the quality of report writing.

> "At least two-thirds are unsatisfactory; ten percent are good. Home circumstances reports haven't improved as much as they ought given National Standards." (Parole Board Member)

The other two Parole Board interviewees, however, were more satisfied with the reports which they received, with one interviewee attributing improvements in quality to National Standards implementation.

Impact of Reports on Decision making

Two interviewees commented that because of the poor information provided in some home circumstances reports, the Board often had to delay the release of a prisoner either through continuing the case for further information or by recommending a forward release date in order that the community based social worker could have more time to make relevant enquires and set up services.

However, the decisions made during the observation period suggest that poor quality information in home circumstances reports is not a major problem. Reference was made to the quality of reports in 23 (8 per cent) out of 290 relevant decisions. In seven of these decisions the Board commented on the high quality of the home circumstances report, mainly because the reports included a well developed release package (four decisions) or the assessments which the report provided were considered to be particularly helpful (three cases). In the other 16 cases the Board commented on the poor quality of the reports. This was generally where the reports provided inadequate information about the level of family support which the prisoner would receive on release (11 decisions) or about other aspects of the release environment. However, the poor quality of these reports directly impacted on the outcome of only five (2 per cent out of 290) decisions. These cases were deferred in order that community based social workers could have more time to prepare a detailed and better researched report.

SUMMARY

The reports in the study sample indicate that National Standards are not always being followed by individual social workers. The responses of social work interviewees from the study sites suggest that this may be due, in part, to divergence of views on the purpose of home circumstances reports and, in part, to difficulties in obtaining information which social workers believed to be essential when making some of the required assessments. Responses also indicate that good intra-agency cooperation may be an essential element in the preparation of high quality home circumstances reports, both in respect of good co-ordination between prison and community based social workers over the timing of report preparation and in obtaining relevant assessments (for example community care assessments from other social work teams).

Parole Board interviewees had mixed views on home circumstances reports. Some were generally satisfied with the reports which they received, citing National Standards as leading to improvements in quality. Others considered that the Standards had had minimal impact and reports were often of poor quality. However, poor quality information in practice (during the observation period) was a factor only in a minority of decisions.

---

[24] During the observation, the Board made explicit reference to information provided by the home circumstances report in 98 (34%) out of 290 relevant decisions. This cannot be taken to imply that information provided by these reports was not important in other decisions as the Board sometimes did not indicate the source of the information which formed the focus of their presentations and/or discussions. Of these 98 decisions, the level of family support was mentioned in 55 (56%) decisions. Other information referred to was as follows: release plans (general) 15 (15%); employment prospects 12 (12%); alcohol problems 7 (7%); social work recommendation of outcome 4 (4%); offending behaviour 2 (2%); drug problems 2(2%); with the following each being mentioned once: early childhood, debt, previous response to supervision, environment to which the prisoner was to return, mental health problems, housing.

PART 2

SERVICES AND DECISION MAKING

CHAPTER FOUR

PRISON SOCIAL WORK SERVICES

INTRODUCTION

Prison social work services are one of the elements of throughcare which do not come within the scope of the National Standards and 100 per cent funding initiative[25]. A key issue arising from Phase One of the research was that social work criminal justice services which did not come within the scope of the policy may be under-resourced and of low priority (McAra, 1998). Although (at the time of writing) prison based social work services are not subject to National Standards, detailed policy and practice guidance, covering the period of the study, are contained in the joint Social Work Services Group and Scottish Prison Service document *Continuity Through Co-operation*[26]. This document states that the key purposes of prison social work are: to assist prisoners to address their offending behaviour; to assess personal and social need; to work with prisoners and their families to assist eventual resettlement in the community; and to develop programmes to address problems commonly presented by prisoners[27].

This chapter explores the views of Parole Board members on the range and quality of services that are available within prison units including the degree to which *Continuity Through Co-operation* and current liaison arrangements have impacted on service development. It also examines prison social work views on factors which impact on service quality.

PAROLE BOARD EXPECTATIONS OF PRISON SOCIAL WORK SERVICES

There was consensus amongst Parole Board interviewees that the key role of the prison social worker should be to assist offenders to address their offending behaviour. A secondary role identified was to refer prisoners to agencies both inside and outside the prison which offered specialist programmes, for example specialist alcohol counselling services.

Addressing Offending

During the observation a high proportion of cases were not recommended for release, in part, because the prisoner had not addressed their offending behaviour (68, or 81 per cent, out of 84 determinate sentence cases not recommended for parole or given an early review). Parole Board interviewees were asked to comment on this pattern and whether there were any links between the outcome of these decisions and the effectiveness of the services which prison social work offered.

Most interviewees did not attribute this pattern of decisions to shortcomings in the social work role, with one interviewee commenting that the services which prison social workers offered were generally extremely effective in assisting prisoners to address their offending (as evidenced by information provided in the dossier and visits made by this Parole Board member to prison units). A number of interviewees recognised, however, that the impact of social work on behaviour and attitudes was often dependent on the motivation of the individual prisoner to change. Absence of such motivation meant that prisoners generally would not be accepted for counselling on specialist programmes, for example sex offender programmes.

> "Prison social workers can on the whole usually get through to a prisoner and are acceptable to them. But the effectiveness of services really does depend on the prisoner going half-way to the social worker." (Parole Board Member)

One Parole Board member commented that prisoners often had negative views of social work especially in cases where the prisoner's children had been taken into care or where the prisoner had been subject to social work supervision as a child. Under these circumstances social workers required to overcome "a good deal of prejudice" before they could work effectively with the prisoner.

---

[25] Prison social work services are currently funded directly by Central Government through the Scottish Prison Service.

[26] The Scottish Office Social Work Services Group/Scottish Prison Service (1989) *Continuity Through Co-operation*, HMSO.

[27] Continuity Through Co-operation: Paragraph 3.2.2. The National Standards document states that *Continuity Through Co-operation* should be read in conjunction with the throughcare Standards (see paragraph 3 The National Standards for Throughcare).

RANGE OF SERVICES

Parole Board Views

A majority of Parole Board interviewees considered that there were variations in the range and quality of social work services in different prison establishments. As a consequence prisoners in certain establishments had better opportunities to address their offending than prisoners elsewhere. Key areas requiring further development were identified as relationship counselling; services for gamblers and anger management work[28].

Even where a broad range of services was available, concern was expressed that sometimes services were over-subscribed and the prisoner could not access them prior to their case being referred to the Board.

> "Why can't they ensure that 'Joe Bloggs' arrives [in prison] and starts the [specialist sex offender] programme in weeks one or two? They'll only get parole if we get positive reports and there are often substantial time delays between arriving at the institution and the prison being able to deliver a place on the programme." (Parole Board Member)

Gaps in services or waiting lists for places created difficulties for the Board when making decisions on individual cases. Interviewees reported that on occasions early review decisions were given in the expectation that the prisoner would undertake some form of counselling prior to the next review. Such cases were often referred back to the Board when no work had been undertaken with the prisoner due to lack of available services.

> "What do we do? Do we stick by our decision which in our view is the right one for the prisoner and it is a prison management problem? Or do we think it probably won't be there but still ask or do we alter our decision....what do we do with the prisoner when it is resources and not them? They can't move on to the next stage, so they have to tread water." (Parole Board Member)

During the observation this issue arose in the discussions of only a minority of cases (15 or 5 per cent out of 290 relevant decisions). This was mainly in respect of the lack of specialist drug counselling services in one particular prison unit. In each of these cases the Board agreed not to recommend the release of the prisoner, as without access to the relevant services such prisoners presented a high risk of re-offending.

Prison Social Work Views

Two of the four prison social workers interviewed considered that their social work units were able to offer, or had access to, a wide range of services. The others, however, commented on the lack of staff to provide services. Two of the study prison units had singleton social work posts and interviewees from these units also stated that workloads made it difficult to develop a wider range of programmes.

Other Services

Both Parole Board and social work interviewees considered that prisoners required a network of services provided by both social work and other agencies to assist them to make progress in custody. Absence of specialist resources meant that social workers often had to "stand in", in most cases where they had little specialist training. Key gaps identified in a number of establishments (including some of the study prison units) were psychiatric and psychological services and specialist drugs and alcohol counselling services.

> "The other resources that people require in prison are not always there. Frequently a particular establishment doesn't do drugs, alcohol or psychological counselling... it is left to the social worker to deal with those things. You really do need [a range] of appropriate resources and other personnel taking part in order to make social work more effective." (Parole Board Member)

There was consensus amongst interviewees that sentence planning could play an important role in facilitating a network of support for a prisoner. Sentence planning however was reported as having faced acute teething troubles. Parole Board interviewees considered that services were often poorly targeted and a requirement was identified for more multi-disciplinary reviews of prisoners and for better inter-agency co-operation in planning for individual need. A number of prison social workers endorsed these views, with one commenting that sentence planning had been virtually abandoned in their establishment.

> "Sentence planning has never worked. We've never really had multi-disciplinary reviews of a person although it started to happen. It's frustrating. Initiatives happen for so long and then they stop and they're not reviewed." (Prison Social Worker).

---

[28] Although anger management work was identified as a key gap in services by a number of interviewees, one interviewee considered that there were too many unevaluated anger management programmes underway.

IMPACT OF CONTINUITY THROUGH CO-OPERATION

Mixed views were expressed by both Parole Board and social work interviewees about the impact of *Continuity Through Co-operation* on the range and quality of prison social work services.

Parole Board Views

Some Parole Board interviewees considered that the quality of services had improved since the implementation of *Continuity Through Co-operation*. This was because social workers were now undertaking more offence focused work with prisoners, as one interviewee commented "they're doing more social work".

However, a concern expressed by a number of interviewees was that there was little consistency in the range of services across prison units nor was there evidence of a structured approach to service development. A contributing factor was that prison social work was often under-resourced.

> "I'm not sure if what is being offered is part of a strategic approach to the prison social work role or whether this is just this month's course. The world and his wife are doing anger management. But I'm not sure if it's been properly evaluated and assessed." (Parole Board Member)

Prison Social Work Views

A number of social work interviewees endorsed Parole Board views on the impact of *Continuity Through Co-operation* on services which prison social work was able to offer. One interviewee commented that it was difficult to take a strategic approach to service development where there was a tension between the funding and management of social work services in prison. (The Scottish Prison Service is currently responsible for funding prison social work whereas local authority social work departments are responsible for managing the services.) Budgeting restrictions were considered to impact adversely on the potential for developing services.

Continuity Through Co-operation states that social workers should be freed to undertake professional tasks and that the development of the prison officer's welfare role has a key role to play in this[29]. There were variations in view amongst prison social workers about the extent to which this had happened.

A number of social workers reported that prison officers in their establishments now undertook all welfare tasks.

> "Yes it's had major impact. Before, social workers were dealing with everything and anything that came through the door and we became immobilised...get prison staff trained in welfare and social work can be left to do social work." (Social Worker)

However, in the prison unit in Bruce arrangements for prison officers to become involved in welfare work had broken down when officers who had undertaken welfare training were replaced by untrained officers.

A common concern was that lack of involvement in welfare tasks might mean that they could miss some potential referrals to the social work unit. Prisoners in the past often approached social workers ostensibly for help with welfare problems when in fact they had much deeper problems they wished to discuss. Now that social workers no longer undertook welfare tasks on a regular basis, such prisoners might find it more difficult to approach them.

LIAISON AND SERVICE DEVELOPMENT

The National Standards state that good liaison arrangements between social work and criminal justice agencies such as the Parole Board and prison services, can enhance the effectiveness of social work services.

Parole Board interviewees had little to say about the effectiveness of liaison arrangements and their impact on service development. Interviewees pointed out that they had the opportunity to raise issues with representatives from both SWSG and SPS at their General Purposes Meetings and most considered that they were always consulted about policy initiatives which had implications for parole. One interviewee commented, however, that SPS did not always consider it necessary to consult the Parole Board over new policy initiatives and that the information which they had about service developments for prisoners often came from individual Board members who had worked in the prison service and/or social work departments.

---

[29] *Continuity Through Co-operation:* Paragraph 3.43.

SUMMARY

Interviewee responses suggest that high quality effective prison based social work services are dependent upon good inter-agency links to facilitate a network of support for the prisoner. Some prison establishments were considered to be better placed than others to provide such a network. A common concern amongst interviewees was that prison social work services were sometimes under-resourced and that there was a need for a more strategically planned approach to service development. Although the implementation of *Continuity Through Co-operation* had promoted a more structured and focused approach to the social work role, little had been done to address the inconsistencies in the range of services available in different prison units.

CHAPTER FIVE

COMMUNITY BASED SOCIAL WORK SERVICES

INTRODUCTION

One of the main objectives of the policy is to improve the quality of the community based element of throughcare services so as to encourage earlier release on licence and compliance with licence requirements. Community based throughcare services include both specialist services which have been developed to tackle particular problems presented by offenders (such as specialist drug and alcohol counselling) as well as the more general supervision which social workers undertake with parolees and life licencees.

This chapter examines Parole Board and social work views on the impact of the policy on the range and effectiveness of services available for prisoners released on parole or life licence.

RANGE OF SERVICES

There was consensus amongst Parole Board and social work interviewees that there was an uneven spread of services across Scotland. Community based social workers from Bruce (the rural study site) and prison social workers commented, in particular, on the difficulties in both developing and accessing services in rural areas. It was recognised by these interviewees that there were insufficient numbers of offenders in such areas to make a range of specialist services viable. Similarly transport difficulties often made it difficult for offenders who lived in the more remote areas of Scotland to access services.

> "Some [social work departments] are better in thinking strategically than others and where they do by and large you'll have all the services there. With others it's not the case. So you might have too much of one [service] and not anything of others." (Parole Board Member)

> "The further up north you go the more difficult it is. If they're going back to the Highlands then you just pray that they've a supportive family." (Prison Social Worker)

Interviewee responses suggest that the implementation of the 100 per cent funding initiative may not have impacted, to date, on the uneven spread of services. There was consensus amongst most interviewees that policy implementation had led to the proliferation of certain services, in particular alcohol and drug counselling services, while other areas were markedly less well developed.

Services identified as requiring further development were specialist services catering for the needs of young adult offenders, women offenders and violent offenders, and psychological counselling and other services for mentally disordered offenders[30]. In addition Parole Board interviewees had specific concerns about the need for more community based sex offender programmes and residential drug rehabilitation placements.

A key concern of all interviewees was the lack of supported and hostel accommodation. Prison social workers in particular commented that some areas in Scotland lacked both types of accommodation. Where a prisoner requiring accommodation was returning to one of these areas, prison social workers had to try and access placements in other local authorities. On occasions difficulties had occurred in determining which of the local authorities should use their grant to fund the placement.

> "There's no accommodation in "B" so if they're from "B" and homeless its "E's" resources that have got to be approached. And then there's the problems of funding, to get someone to be responsible for funding a residential placement." (Prison Social Worker)

The gaps in services identified by interviewees would become of particular significance to parole decision making, if there were large numbers of cases where the Board could not recommend the release of a prisoner because of the lack of a specific community based social work resource. During the observation period however, such delays in release occurred in only a minority of decisions (9 or 3 per cent out of 290 relevant decisions), discussed in more detail in Chapter Seven.

---

[30] A particular concern of prison social workers was that no one agency was willing to take responsibility for mentally disordered offenders and that greater clarification was required as to which agency should take the lead role (whether it be the Health Board or social work department). Such cases were reported as involving a great deal of "brokering" between agencies.

Role of the Independent Sector

The National Standards state that local authorities must consider the contribution that the independent sector can make to the provision of offender services[31]. Parole Board and social work interviewees were asked to comment on the range of services which this sector offered.

There were variations in view about the role of the independent sector in the provision of services. A number of interviewees were generally satisfied. However others commented that such agencies tended to be "fighting over the same clients" and consequently the range of services was small. A further concern was that the independent sector was not always sufficiently rigorous in monitoring and evaluating its own performance. While most Parole Board and social work interviewees considered that the independent sector had a vital role to play in providing services which were not available in the statutory sector, there was concern that their role was limited because the independent sector tended to be resource rather than needs led:

> "It's poor for all sorts of reasons. Most of the facilities that are available .. are provided by voluntary organisations who are themselves limited in terms of what they can do on the basis of resources. Too often what is available is not there on the basis of need but how you get the money." (Parole Board Member)

Interviewees considered that there was scope for the independent sector to develop a much wider support network for released prisoners. A particular need was identified for more out of hours and weekend support.

Demand for Services

One measure of the Board's requirements for services would be the additional requirements which they insert into parole and life licences. During the observation period the Board inserted these into the licences of 50 prisoners. A minority of these were to be included in the prisoner's licence "at the discretion of the supervising officer".

During interview Board members stated that they inserted additional requirements into licences where they had concerns about the level of risk that a prisoner posed. The additional requirements were therefore included in the licence as a means of risk management. Interviewees commented that they rarely had any information about whether the additional requirements were put into practice unless the case was referred to the Board for consideration of recall.

> "They're often to maintain low risk of re-offending. I don't know if they're put into practice. They ought to be but we never hear." (Parole Board Member)

It was the expectation of the Board that additional requirements in licences would give the licencee the opportunity to make use of specialist resources in addition to the types of counselling which supervising officers were able to offer as part of the normal requirements of statutory supervision. One interviewee commented, however, that when making recommendations for additional requirements they were conscious of weighing the need for greater control over the prisoner in the community against the scarce level of resources. Others stated that they would recommend additional requirements even if they were not sure whether the services they requested were available. There was, however, an expectation that if the requested services were not available, then the case would be referred back to the Board.

The additional requirements inserted into licences during the observation are summarised in Table 5.1 .

Table 5.1: Additional Requirements in Licence

Additional Requirement	Number
Alcohol Counselling	33
Drug Counselling	21
Supported Accommodation	9
Psychological Counselling	7
Anger Management Counselling	2
Residence Specified (e.g. Not to reside with Spouse)	4
Social Skills Counselling	2
Counselling on Offending	1
Place on Sex Offender Programme	1

---

[31] *National Objectives and Standards:* Part 1 General Issues Paragraph 94.

Importantly what this table indicates is that services for which there is greatest demand (alcohol and drug counselling) are the ones which interviewees identified as being services which had proliferated since National Standards implementation. Although all interviewees focused on lack of suitable accommodation as being a key gap in services, the demand for places is relatively low. However, the prisoners who require accommodation are often those whom the Board perceives to be high risk (mainly sex offenders and prisoners with mental health problems: see Chapter Seven for discussion of the importance of social work services for high risk prisoners). This may account for the Board's sensitivity towards gaps in this type of service.

QUALITY OF COMMUNITY BASED SUPERVISION

Parole Board Views

A number of Parole Board interviewees commented that they had very little information about the content of parole supervision. In general, the Board only received information about progress of parolees in cases where problems had arisen and the licencee was being referred for consideration of recall. This made it difficult for interviewees to assess the impact of the Standards. One interviewee did however comment that the quality of community based supervision had improved since National Standards implementation. They felt that social workers were now more focused in their approach to supervision and undertook more work on offending behaviour.

A key concern of some Parole Board interviewees was that supervising officers did not always appear to understand the expectations of the Board in respect of contact with the offender and reporting frequency (in respect of life licencees). For example where the Board requested quarterly reporting they would expect the supervising officer to have more frequent contact than this (frequency of reporting was considered to enhance the controlling elements of a licence). In the Board's experience, supervising officers often only contacted life licencees when a report was required. Similar views were expressed by Parole Board interviewees at Phase One of the research programme (McAra, 1998), suggesting that there has been little change over the two year period between the Phase One research and this study.

Community based Social Work Views

Social workers from two of the study sites (Bruce and Wallace) commented that they lacked experience in supervising parolees and life licencees as their team had to deal with only one or two cases per year. As they were not experienced in supervising this type of client they did not feel qualified to respond to questions about the impact of Standards on supervision.

Other interviewees considered that the quality of supervision had improved since the implementation of National Standards. Improvements were linked to a more structured approach to supervision and more offence focused work. A number of social workers commented, however, that the key change introduced by National Standards was that offenders were now considered a priority group:

> "We can actually say to people you have...a right to be seen, a right to my time. In the past you might have had to leave an offender when other priorities came along. When there were mixed case loads... they were probably not seen... Offender work is no longer the bottom of the heap." (Community based Social Worker)

SUMMARY

Interviewee responses indicate that the impact of the policy on the range and effectiveness of community based social work services has been somewhat uneven. While the policy appears to have facilitated the development of a number of services such as alcohol counselling, significant gaps remain.

Some improvements in the quality of supervision of licencees were discerned by interviewees. However, the Parole Board did not appear to have much information about the nature of supervision.

From interviewee responses, it would appear that a high quality and effective community based social work service is associated with well planned services and good inter- and intra-agency co-ordination. Policy implementation according to these interviewees has yet to result in such a service being delivered in all areas.

CHAPTER SIX

IMPACT OF SOCIAL WORK SERVICES ON DECISION MAKING: PAROLE BOARD VIEWS

INTRODUCTION

A key aim of the National Standards is to encourage the earlier release of prisoners on licence. In order to achieve this aim standards of service and 100 per cent funding have been targeted on the community based element of throughcare. The introduction to the Standards cites the then Secretary of State's Howard League speech (1988) in which he stated that prisons are not the ideal place in which to teach an offender to live a normal and law-abiding life[32]. The model of social work practice which underpins the Standards holds that rehabilitation of offenders can be better effected within a community setting and that supervision which comprises elements of both care and control can have a positive impact on offending behaviour.

The impact of the National Standards on Parole Board decision making is likely to be affected by the extent to which the Parole Board deem the reformative and rehabilitative framework of the Standards to be an appropriate model for dealing with more serious and persistent offenders. An important indicator of successful policy implementation would be the extent to which consideration of community based services and supervision was a key focus in decisions made to recommend parole or release on life licence. Parole Board members were asked about their objectives when making parole decisions, including those for high risk offender groups, and whether arrangements for policy implementation had resulted in any changes in their decision making practice.

AIMS IN DECISION MAKING

During interview Parole Board members were willing to endorse the objectives of statutory supervision as set out in the National Standards, in particular the statement that supervision should assist offenders to reduce their risk of re-offending and to adhere to their licence conditions.

A common perception amongst interviewees was that parole and release on life licence were mechanisms for allowing certain prisoners to continue their sentence within a community based setting but that whilst on licence these prisoners should make constructive use of their time in rebuilding links with the community. Parole was viewed therefore as a means of assisting reintegration but also of ensuring control of behaviour. Control was to be achieved through regular supervision and also through the sanction of recall.

> "It's a means for identifying those who can be released early and serve their sentence in the community in such a way as a) they don't re-offend; and b) use their time constructively i.e. its not just a mechanism for sentence shortening." (Parole Board Member)

> "It's balancing the ultimate safety of keeping someone who's a proven offender in custody and a recognition that ultimately they will have to go out into the community. It's balancing care and control, letting someone show that they can make it but if they can't we have some control in bringing them back." (Parole Board Member)

Interviewee responses suggest, however, that the Parole Board takes different factors into account when making decisions on determinate and indeterminate sentence (lifer) cases.

DETERMINATE SENTENCE CASES: FACTORS TAKEN INTO ACCOUNT

There was consensus amongst Parole Board interviewees that risk of re-offending was the main factor which they took into account in considering which prisoners were suitable for release on parole.

> "My primary concern is what I assess to be the risk of re-offending and since that is the main question I'm asking myself I read everything in the dossier to see what indicates low risk and what indicates high risk." (Parole Board Member)

---

[32] *National Objectives and Standards:* Introduction Paragraph 2.

All Parole Board members interviewed indicated that they assessed risk of re-offending in a similar way. Factors commonly mentioned as indicators of risk were: the nature and circumstances of the current offence; the number and pattern of previous convictions; the extent to which the offender had addressed their offending behaviour (see below), and any related or underlying problems such as drug or alcohol misuse; the level of support the offender would have on release from family or other significant relationships; and plans for managing time in the community in respect of employment, educational opportunities or constructive leisure activities.

Addressing offending was linked by interviewees to both a change in attitude on the part of the prisoner (through acceptance of responsibility for the offence, by not minimising their role in the offence and expressions of remorse) and efforts made by the prisoner to address problems which were directly associated with offending.

> "It's whether or not they minimise the offence, whether they express genuine remorse. If the offence is linked to addictions problems whether they have addressed it. If there is evidence of change in the dossier."
> (Parole Board Member)

One interviewee considered that the Parole Board represented the public and that, as a Board member, it was their duty to reflect public attitudes towards different types of crime when making assessments of risk.

The key indicators of risk mentioned by the Board in interview are summarised in Table 6.1.

Table 6.1: Indicators of Risk

Level Of Risk	Past Behaviour	Change In Custody	Future Structures
	Response of Criminal Justice System	Services and Prisoner Responsibility	Services, relationships, prospects
High	High number of previous convictions Increasing severity or persistence	*Failure to address offending* *Failure to address addictions*	Lack of support/poor relationships *Unstructured time*
Low	Low number of previous convictions	*Addressed offending* *Addressed addictions*	Supportive relationships *Structured time*

Factors on which social work services can impact are in italics.

Social work services can only impact on some of these indicators (these indicators are highlighted in italics), others lie beyond its scope, for example the number of previous convictions or the strength of family or other significant relationships[33]. Importantly, the indicators suggest that community based social work services may only have a limited role to play in risk reduction, by assisting the prisoner to develop a coherent plan for managing their time in the community. By contrast, the indicators linked to change in custody highlight the important role which effective prison social work services could play in risk reduction. As highlighted in Chapter Four, interviewees did, however, recognise that the level of impact of such services was dependent upon the prisoner's own motivation to change, with one view being that the highest risk prisoners were the least tractable. In this respect changes in the range and quality of prison social work services might provide greater opportunities for prisoners to address their problems but this would only impact on the decision making practice of the Board where prisoners themselves chose to make use of these opportunities.

Impact of Risk Assessments on Decision making

There was consensus amongst interviewees that where prisoners had made little effort to address their offending during their time in custody, they were not likely to be recommended for parole. Level of risk had therefore to be reduced prior to release into the community, rather than reduced or managed in a non-custodial setting through the provision of high quality community based social work services. This would suggest that change in custody takes precedence over future structures in decisions made to recommend release on parole.

---

[33] The supplement to the National Standards document *(Social Work Supervision Towards Effective Policy and Practice)* states that social work supervision should focus, in part, on addressing underlying problems, including family relationship problems. The Board however was concerned about the bond between the prisoner and their family, a factor which social work may not be able to impact directly upon.

"No matter how good the release package they're not likely to get parole if the level of risk hasn't changed. In the dossier I'm looking for change in the level of risk. Even if the SCRO print-out goes to many pages but that person's managed to convince the authors of the various reports that I'm a changed person, I've refocused - I can live with that. If they haven't changed I'm fairly sceptical." (Parole Board Member)

One exception to this general pattern was high risk prisoners who only had a short period of parole available before their two-thirds of sentence date. Interviewees agreed that such prisoners might be recommended for parole in order to ensure that the prisoner was released into a controlled environment rather than being released at their two-thirds date with no controls at all. Such prisoners were described by interviewees as "on balance" cases and were considered to be the most difficult type of case on which to take a decision.

"For example a sex offender who's not addressed their offending behaviour. Do we keep him in to the last possible moment to protect the public or let him out in the last four months to some social work supervision? If we do the latter, at least we have a hold on him if only to know where he is, to indicate to him that there is a controlling element. We never come to that decision lightly." (Parole Board Member)

Interviewee responses suggest that the Board expects social work to fulfil a "policing" function under these circumstances, with rehabilitation or reintegration of the prisoner taking a secondary role.

" It's better to have some supervision to keep tracks on them than open the door and away they go. They might be high risk but it's the best way of controlling risk." (Parole Board Member)

INDETERMINATE SENTENCE CASES: FACTORS TAKEN INTO ACCOUNT

There was consensus amongst Parole Board interviewees, that when making decisions on indeterminate sentence cases (lifers) that the Board looked for a period of sustained progress in custody and made assessments of the extent to which prisoners had developed or changed.

"A period of improvement and stability, with most lifers it is possible to see this because of the length of time they get before they come to us. It is quite clear the changes that have been made from the daft drunken boy to the very mature person with an Open University degree". (Parole Board Member)

Key measures of progress were identified as: response to testing, for example in open conditions, on home-leaves, or on a work placement in the community, and progress in addressing addiction (or other significant) problems. Although some of these measures are similar to the risk indicators highlighted above in relation to determinate sentence cases, when discussing lifers, interviewees did not associate these measures with levels of risk. Unlike determinate sentence cases, an assessment of risk was believed to be inappropriate for most lifers, due to the "one-off" nature of the offence.

"The normal criterion of risk is less appropriate. Lifers are some of the least dangerous people. I worry less about them than I do about sex offenders." (Parole Board Member)

Interviewees did, however, comment that when deliberating on indeterminate sentence cases they required to balance their own perceptions of the case with what they considered the public's view of life sentence prisoners to be (namely that these prisoners were highly dangerous and required close control on release).

While the focus on progress in custody in these cases highlights the potential for effective prison based social work services to impact on decision-making, interviewee responses suggest that community based social work services will have a less important role to play.

IMPACT OF NATIONAL STANDARDS ON DECISION MAKING

The model of social work practice in the National Standards is premised on the belief that risk can be effectively managed in a community based setting where social workers provide the correct balance of care and control. Parole Board interviewees were asked whether arrangements for implementing the policy had encouraged them to release a greater number of prisoners on licence at an earlier stage. As highlighted in Chapter Five, some Parole Board interviewees had not discerned any major changes in the quality of community based services since policy implementation. These interviewees commented that it was therefore unlikely that policy implementation would have impacted on the decisions which they took. Even interviewees who had a more optimistic view of the impact of the policy on service quality, were equivocal as to whether improvements in services *in themselves* would be sufficient to guarantee a parole recommendation in every "on balance" case.

"I doubt it. I'm not sure that National Standards have made a colossal impact (on decision making). I buy the theory totally but I've a gut feeling that we've not seen a massive improvement in that area." (Parole Board Member)

One interviewee considered that more feedback on the outcome of supervision might make the Board more willing to release some higher risk offenders on licence at an earlier stage.

"We do try to take the risks that National Standards would urge us but what we lack is appropriate feedback. If we've released a sex offender and they've made it and they've done it because a specific resource is available in the community to which they've gone as a condition and it's worked - that is the kind of information we need - there is no statistical information, no analysis of success rates - we'd be more willing to take that kind of risk if we had more information." (Parole Board Member)

However, this view was not shared by all interviewees, with one commenting that the process of supervision was entirely a matter for the social work department and, as a consequence, greater feedback on the progress of individual orders would not be welcomed.

A common view was that the number of high risk cases released for short periods of parole was likely to be even smaller in the future because of changes introduced by the Prisoners and Criminal Proceedings (Scotland) Act 1993. Under the arrangements introduced by this Act, prisoners serving four years or more and who do not get parole will be on licence from their two-thirds of sentence date (previously the date at which prisoners were automatically released without supervision) until the end of their sentence. Parole Board interviewees agreed that the use of short periods of parole to control prisoners are less likely to be an attractive option to the Board when they know that the prisoners will automatically be on licence on release at their two-thirds date.

"If they're high risk they'll be less likely to get parole. If we know that the person will be on licence from two-thirds until the end of sentence, they'll be a controlled risk... If they've not addressed their offending then frankly six months in the community would make little difference but six months more in prison, we know that they're not going to offend so let's keep him there." (Parole Board Member)

SUMMARY

Parole Board interviewee responses indicate that release on licence for both determinate and indeterminate sentence cases is dependent primarily on progress or change in custody. Given the importance which interviewees attached to these criteria, it would be unlikely that a policy targeting community based services could have a major impact on decisions which are made. Even interviewees who had discerned a change in the quality of community based services since policy implementation did not consider that this had impacted on the decision making practice of the Board.

However, a common view was that community based social work services could have a key role to play in the decisions made on some high risk determinate sentence cases with short periods of parole available. The role of social work under these circumstances was, primarily, one of control rather than rehabilitation. While more serious and persistent offenders are a key policy target group, interviewees did point out that the number of such cases which were suitable for a short period of parole was extremely small and was the hardest type of case on which to make a decision (confirmed by the observation data which are discussed in more detail in Chapter Seven).

Interviewee responses suggest that successful policy implementation would, in part, require a shift in the perspective of the Board about the context in which risk can be most effectively reduced. Changing their decision making practice would require the Board to take what, in their view, would be greater "risks" when considering the types of case which could be "safely" released into the community.

Decisions on early release are the prerogative of the full Parole Board. It is important, therefore, to consider the extent to which the practice of the Board (as observed during the fieldwork period) reflects the perceptions of the four Parole Board members who were interviewed. This will be examined in more detail in the following chapters.

CHAPTER SEVEN

DECISION MAKING PRACTICE: SOCIAL WORK IMPACT CASES

INTRODUCTION

One of the main objectives of the policy is to enable more serious and persistent offenders to be dealt with in a non-custodial setting. The overall aim in respect of throughcare is to improve the quality of supervision of released prisoners so as to encourage earlier release on licence. In order to do this 100 percent funding and National Standards have been targeted on the community based element of throughcare provision. The responses of Parole Board interviewees suggest, however, that community based social work services are only likely to have a key role to play in decisions made on a small number of high risk cases.

As no base-line study was undertaken, it is not possible to determine, through analysis of the decision making patterns alone, whether any substantial *change* in decision making has occurred as a result of policy implementation. However, a key measure of how the policy was impacting on decision making at the time of the research would be the extent to which consideration of services which community based social work could offer was a contributory factor in decisions to recommend (provisional) release.

During the observation the Board considered 253 cases for which a recommendation for (provisional) release was a potential outcome[34]. Of these 216 (85 per cent) were determinate and 37 (15 per cent) were indeterminate sentence cases. However, in only 39 (15 per cent) of these cases (all determinate sentence prisoners) were factors relating to community based social work services given as contributing *reasons* for the decisions that were made (impact cases).

This chapter compares the characteristics of the impact cases with the other determinate sentence cases in the observation sample[35] (for which social work services did not impact on outcome), and considers the implications of the decision making patterns in relation to impact cases, for successful policy implementation.

CHARACTERISTICS OF CASES

The characteristics of the impact cases differed in a number of important ways from the other determinate sentence cases (non-impact cases) in the observation sample[36]. Firstly there was a much higher proportion of sex offenders in the impact sample (21 per cent as compared with 8 per cent of the non-impact cases). Secondly a much smaller proportion of the impact sample was at first review for parole purposes (38 per cent as compared with 60 per cent of the non-impact sample) with a correspondingly higher proportion of impact cases at third or later review (31 per cent as compared with 10 per cent of non-impact cases). This was also reflected in the higher proportion of impact cases with shorter periods of parole available (72 per cent as compared with 55 per cent of non-impact cases). The differences between the samples are given in more detail in the following tables.

Table 7.1: Impact and Non-Impact Cases: Offence

Offence	Impact Cases Percent (n=39)		Non-Impact Cases Percent (n=177)	
Violence	56	(22)	63	(112)
Sex	21	(8)	8	(15)
Misuse Of Drugs Act	13	(5)	18	(31)
Dishonesty	8	(3)	8	(14)
Road Traffic Act	3	(1)	-	
Other	-		3	(5)

Percentages do not add up to 100 because of rounding
Shaded areas: key differences
Numbers in brackets: actual number of cases

---

[34] This excludes: cases which were referred for the Board to note information only (8 cases); licence change cases (3 cases), and cases referred for consideration of recall (47 cases). In none of these cases was a (provisional) release decision a possible outcome.

[35] The characteristics of the impact cases are not compared with indeterminate sentence cases in this chapter. Both interviewee responses and the decision-making patterns during the observation period, confirm that the Board uses a different set of criteria when making decisions on the release of lifers from the criteria taken into account in parole (determinate) sentence cases.

[36] This section of the chapter focuses on the key *differences* between the samples. Other details about the samples are included in the report at Annex III.

Table 7.2: Impact and Non-Impact Cases: Review Number

Review Number	Impact Cases Percent (n=39)		Non-Impact Cases Percent (n=177)	
First	38	(15)	60	(107)
Second	31	(12)	29	(52)
Third Or Later	31	(12)	10	(18)

Percentages do not add up to 100 because of rounding
Shaded areas: key differences
Numbers in brackets: actual number of cases

Table 7.3 Impact and Non-Impact Cases: Parole Available

Parole Available	Impact Cases Percent (n=39)		Non-Impact Cases Percent (n=177)	
Less Than 1 Year	72	(28)	55	(98)
1 Year +	28	(11)	45	(79)

Shaded areas: key differences
Numbers in brackets: actual number of cases

DECISION MAKING PATTERNS: IMPACT CASES

Social work services featured in two distinct ways in the reasons given for outcome in impact cases: firstly, cases where the Board considered that the prisoner would benefit from a period of social work supervision (12 cases); secondly, cases where the availability of a social work resource (or other specialist service provided by the independent sector) was a key element in the decision whether (or not) to recommend release on parole (23 cases). In four cases both reasons were given.

Table 7.4: Impact Cases: Reasons for Outcome

Reason	Number (n=39)
Benefit from Supervision	12
Availability of Social Work Resource	23
Both	4

Benefit from Supervision

The Board gave two main reasons as to why cases would benefit from social work supervision: for eight cases the period of supervision was considered essential as a means of *risk management* (this includes the four cases in which consideration of the availability of social work services was also an important consideration); for a further three cases the period of supervision was recommended to assist the prisoner to *reintegrate into the community*.[37]

---

[37] In five cases no explanation was explicitly given by the Board as to why the prisoner would benefit from supervision. However in two of these cases additional reasons were given by the Board for outcome which were confirmed in interview to be indicators of low risk of re-offending. In a further case additional reasons related to features of the case which were confirmed in interview to be indicators of high risk. However, the Board did not explicitly link supervision to risk management in the reasons given for this case and therefore it is not included in the section on supervision as risk management. In a further two cases no additional reasons were given for outcome.

Supervision as Risk Management

Cases where a period of supervision was considered to be necessary in order to minimise the risk of re-offending, were those of prisoners who had either failed to address their offending behaviour or addiction problems during time spent in custody, and/or because of the nature of their offence (mostly violent or sex offences).[38.] A short period on parole was recommended to ensure that the prisoner was released to some form of control rather than being released unconditionally at their two-thirds of sentence date.

"I'm not confident that he wouldn't repeat the Road Traffic Act offence - a possible obsession with cars. For this reason would benefit from a short period of supervision."

(Transcript: Male prisoner, aged 19, serving short term sentence for Road Traffic Act Offences, with period of less than one year available for parole)

"Release ...benefit from supervision, it is essential in the public interest, risk of re-offending."

(Transcript: Male prisoner, aged 59, serving long term sentence for sex offences, with a period of less than one year available for parole)

As highlighted in Chapter Six, Parole Board interviewees considered that this type of high risk case was the most difficult on which to make a decision. This is reflected in the discussions on three of these eight cases, in which Board members had differing views as to whether the case presented too great a risk to warrant parole. Indeed two of the cases were eventually recommended for early release by a majority vote.

"- In prison he gives the impression of knuckling down but we've not seen any change in attitude towards his wife (the victim).

- I share your anxieties but it's for the benefit of all that he goes out with supervision rather than not.

- He would respond well to social work."

(Transcript: Male prisoner aged 35, serving long term sentence for violent offences, at second review with a period of less than one year available for parole.)

Although the numbers are extremely small, the decision making patterns in respect of these cases confirm interviewees' perceptions that the Board is prepared to release some of the most high risk prisoners to a short period of social work supervision. (All of these cases were at their last review for parole purposes).

Supervision to Assist Reintegration

Cases where social work supervision was intended to assist the prisoner to reintegrate into the community, were those of prisoners nearing the end of extremely long sentences[39]. Supervision was necessary as the length of time which such prisoners had spent in custody was considered to have led to a deterioration in their links both to their families and to the communities to which they would be returning.

"The full four months (of parole available). He's coming to the end of his longest custodial sentence and supervision will help him to reintegrate into his home and into the community."

(Transcript: Male prisoner aged 44, serving long term sentence for violent offences with a period of less than one year available for parole)

The Availability of Social Work Resources

In 27 impact cases the availability (or lack) of a specific social work resource was one of the main reasons given for outcome. (These cases comprise the 23 cases for which the availability of the social work resource was the only aspect of social work services mentioned, and the four cases where the Board considered that the prisoner would also benefit from supervision as a means of risk management, discussed in detail above.)

Services in Place

In 18 (67 per cent) of these 27 cases social workers had both identified specialist resources in the community and made enquiries about the availability of such placements, *prior* to the case coming to the Board[40]. The types of services which were key to outcome in these cases and the types of prisoner with which they were associated are described in the following table.

---

[38] Cases benefiting from supervision as means of risk management comprise prisoners convicted of: violent offences (4); sex offences (3); and Road Traffic Act Offences (1).

[39] These cases comprise: two prisoners convicted of violent offences and one prisoner convicted of Misuse of Drugs Act offences.

[40] This includes the four cases mentioned above in which benefit from supervision was also an important consideration.

Table 7.5: Impact Cases: Services Key to Outcome

Service	Offence
Alcohol Counselling	Violence 8 Sex 2 Dishonesties 1
Supported Accommodation	Violence 5 Sex 3
Drug Counselling	Misuse of Drugs Act 2 Violence 1
Action Plan (Unspecified)	Sex 1
Sex Offender Project	Sex 1
Psychological Counselling	Sex 2 Violence 1
Employment Training	Violence 1

Violence (n=10), Sex (n=5), MDA (n=2), Dishonesties (n=1)
Numbers add up to more than 18 as more than one service was mentioned in some cases

All of these 18 cases received a positive outcome with 14 being recommended for parole and four for a forward release date (the forward date was given in three of these cases to allow a period of counselling and/or training for freedom to be completed prior to release, and, in one case, to ensure the period of supervision in the community was short in order to "maximise public protection").

Services Not in Place

In the remaining nine cases (of the 27 where the availability of services impacted on outcome), social work services had not been put in place by the time that the case was considered by the Board and this contributed to delays in release[41].

The main reasons for services not being in place were as follows: the Parole Board identified a need for specialist counselling which had been overlooked by social workers (3 cases); social workers had assessed needs prior to the case coming to the Board but placements had not been set up (3 cases)[42]; social workers had been unable to secure funding for a residential drug rehabilitation placement considered by the Board to be essential to reduce risk of re-offending (one case); social workers had experienced difficulties in arranging supported accommodation for "difficult" offenders (two sex offenders, one of whom was mentally disordered[43]).

In six of these nine cases, the Board recommended a forward release date (rather than parole) in order that social workers could have more time to arrange services. A further two cases were continued to give social workers more time to set up relevant placements. However, in one high risk case (that of a sex offender requiring supported accommodation) difficulties in setting up a placement contributed to the decision not to recommend parole at current review.

IMPLICATIONS OF DECISION MAKING PATTERNS

The impact sample indicates that social work services currently have a key role to play in only a small proportion of the cases with which the Board deals. The differences between this sample and the remaining non-impact determinate sentence cases suggest that social work services may be particularly important for sex

---

[41] These cases comprise prisoners convicted of: violent offences (4); sex offences (2), Misuse of Drugs Act offences (2); and dishonesties (1).

[42] In two of these cases the Parole Board attributed the failure to set up placements to poor liaison between the prison social worker and community based social workers.

[43] In the case of the sex offender without mental health problems, supported accommodation agencies were reported as being unwilling to accept the case due to the nature of the offence.
In the case of the sex offender who was also mentally disordered, supported accommodation agencies were reported to be reluctant to accept the case as the prisoner had a history of setting fire to their cell. A further concern in this case was poor inter-agency collaboration between social work and psychiatric services. The Health Board in the area to which the prisoner was to return was reported as being unwilling to become involved with the case and Parole Board members were uncertain as to whether or not it was SPS or social work who should take the lead role in making arrangements for psychiatric assessment of need. The Board agreed to continue the case in order to allow the prison social worker and psychiatrist more time to develop a package of care.

offenders on release into the community; and/or for cases rejected for parole on a number of previous occasions but which now only have a short period of time before the two-thirds of sentence date (at which time under the old arrangements for parole the prisoner would be released unconditionally).

Importantly however, in almost all of the impact cases (37 or 95 per cent of impact cases) additional reasons were given for decisions as summarised in the following table.

Table 7.6: Impact Cases: Additional Reasons

Social Work Impact	Low Risk Features (n=24)	High Risk Features (n=13)	Total Number of Cases (n=37)
Benefit from supervision	2	1	3
Benefit from supervision: risk management	-	4	4
Benefit from supervision: assist reintegration	3	-	3
Social work resource available	13	1	14
Social work resource not available	6	3	9
Benefit from supervision: risk management and social work resource available	-	4	4

Shaded area in low risk column: five cases recommended for positive outcomes; one case continued to enable placement to be set up
Shaded area in high risk column: 1 case recommended for positive outcome; one case continued to enable placement to be set up; 1 case not recommended for release
Numbers in non-shaded areas: cases either recommended for parole or forward release date

For 24 cases the additional reasons related to positive features of the case, which were confirmed by interviewees to be indicators of low risk (the prisoner had addressed their offending and/or addiction problems; had made good progress in custody and/or had a supportive family). As highlighted in Chapter Six, Parole Board interviewees commented that determinate sentence cases with such low risk features would generally be recommended for release. As these 24 cases had features which would make a release recommendation a likely outcome (*in addition* to the involvement of community based social work resources), it could be argued that the availability of the social work resource had a *contributory* but not necessarily a pivotal role to play in the decision.

In a further 13 cases, however, the additional reasons given by the Board related to features of the case which were confirmed in interview to be indicators of high risk (the prisoner had failed to address their offending behaviour and/or addiction problems). There was consensus amongst Parole Board interviewees that high risk cases would not generally be recommended for parole. It could therefore be argued that for the high risk cases in the impact sample, the availability of social work services/supervision was one of the *crucial* elements in the decision whether or not to recommend early release.

SUMMARY

As highlighted in the introduction to this chapter, a key policy aim is to enable more serious and persistent offenders to be dealt with in a non-custodial setting. It is difficult to conclude, at this stage, that the small number of high risk cases with positive outcomes in the impact sample, represents a major success for the policy. If the policy were impacting on decision making (in the manner suggested by the policy) one might expect that the Board would have greater confidence in recommending release for *larger* numbers of high risk cases. Furthermore all of the high risk impact cases were at their final review for parole purposes. In this respect the policy aim of encouraging release on licence at an *earlier* stage is not currently being fulfilled.

The decisions made on the impact sample indicate that the Board considers that social work services may be particularly important for offenders coming to the end of a long sentence to assist them reintegrate into the community; sex offenders on release into the community; and a small number of high risk cases with short periods available for parole. However, the decision making patterns also show that social work services are more likely to impact on decisions where services have been put in place *prior* to the case coming before the Board. Failure to do so can be an impediment to early release.

If social work services can facilitate the release of a small group of often high risk prisoners the key question becomes why services appear to be less important for other types of high risk case (in the non-impact sample). This issue will be explored in the next chapter.

CHAPTER EIGHT

DECISION MAKING PRACTICE: NON-IMPACT AND INDETERMINATE SENTENCE CASES

INTRODUCTION

Parole Board interviewees suggested that community based social work services were only likely to have a key role to play in decisions made on a small number of high risk cases. These views were confirmed, in part, by the types of cases considered during the observation where the availability of social work resources impacted on outcome.

This chapter examines the remainder of the determinate and indeterminate sentence cases for which community based social work services did not impact on outcome and explores the implications of the decision making patterns for successful policy implementation.

DETERMINATE SENTENCE CASES

There were 177 determinate sentence cases[44] where consideration of social work services did not feature in the reasons given by the Board for decisions made (non-impact cases)[45], compared with 39 determinate sentence cases where services did feature. Most of the cases in the non-impact sample (165 or 93 per cent) were referred for consideration of release with a smaller number (12 or 7 per cent) being referred for consideration of an adverse development (adverse development cases are considered in more detail at the end of the chapter)[46].

As noted in Chapter Seven, the key differences between the non-impact and impact cases were: there was a smaller proportion of sex offenders in the non-impact cases; a higher proportion of non-impact cases were at first review for parole purposes; and a higher proportion of non-impact cases had longer periods of parole available (one year or more). (The characteristics of the non-impact sample are described in more detail in Annex III.)

Consideration of Release

The decision making patterns in relation to the determinate sentence non-impact cases referred for consideration of release, reflect Parole Board interviewees' concerns with risk of re-offending. Both the discussions and the main reasons given for outcome are framed by the indicators of risk highlighted in Chapter Six.

Outcomes

Half of the non-impact cases received a negative outcome, with 56 (34 per cent) not being recommended for release at current review and 27 (16 per cent) recommended for an early review. Of the other non-impact cases, 71 (43 per cent) received a decision either to recommend parole or a forward release date and a further 11 cases were continued. The outcomes for cases are summarised in the following table[47].

Table 8.1: Non-Impact Cases: Outcome

Outcome	Percent (n=165)	
Parole/Forward Date	43	(71)
Early Review	16	(27)
Not Release	34	(56)
Continuation	7	(11)

Percentages do not add up to 100 because of rounding
Numbers in brackets: actual number of cases.

---

[44] This excludes three cases referred for the Board to note information and one licence change case.

[45] This should not be taken to mean that social work services were not mentioned in the presentation or discussions of cases but only that they did not have an impact on the decision that was eventually reached.

[46] Fourteen of the cases were referred back to the Board within the fieldwork period. Most had been continued for further information at an earlier meeting and were being re-referred because the required information was available (11 cases). In three cases, where the prisoner had been recommended for parole or a forward release date at first referral, the case was re-referred because of an adverse development (see detailed discussion of this type of referral below).

[47] Most cases were continued because the Board required further information in order to make a better assessment of the prisoner's risk of re-offending (5 cases) or the extent of their mental health (3 cases), addiction or other problems (3 cases). Deficiencies in information provided by social work were the primary reason given for the continuation in five of these cases (updated reports were required in four out of these five cases and signed social work reports in the other case).

Positive Outcomes

The types of reasons given for cases in which parole or a forward date was recommended are summarised in Table 8.2

Table 8.2: Non-Impact Cases: Reasons for Positive Outcomes

Context	Reason	Percent (n=71)	
Past Behaviour	Low No. Previous Convictions/1st Custodial	32	(23)
	Good Response to Previous Supervision	4	(3)
	Addressed Offending/Low Risk	44	(31)
	Not Addressed Offending/High Risk	4	(3)
Change in Custody	Addressed Addictions/No Addiction Problems	31	(22)
	Addiction Problems	6	(4)
	Addressed Anger Control Problems	3	(2)
	Good Conduct in Custody/Response to Testing	11	(8)
	Poor Conduct/Response to Testing	6	(4)
	Positive Change (Unspecified	15	(11)
	Good Use of Facilities	8	(6)
(Forward Date Only)	To Allow for Further Testing/Complete TFF *	8	(6)
(Forward Date Only)	To Allow Counselling to Begin/Complete	18	(13)
(Forward Date Only)	Incentive to Change	6	(4)
	Good Family Support	42	(30)
	Poor Family Support	6	(4)
Future Structures	Good Employment Prospects	24	(17)
	Good Accommodation Plans	1	(1)
	Good Release Plans (not linked to social work services)	3	(2)
Other	Compassionate	1	(1)

Percentages add up to more than 100 as more than one reason was given in most cases
Shaded areas: most frequently mentioned reasons
Numbers in brackets: actual number of cases
* Training for Freedom

Although a wide range of reasons was given by the Board for positive outcomes, the reasons most frequently given were that the prisoner had: addressed their offending behaviour during time spent in custody and/ or was at low risk of re-offending (evidenced by not minimising their role in the offence and/or expressions of remorse); supportive family or other relationships; a low number of previous convictions or it was their first custodial sentence ; and the prisoner had either made efforts to address their addiction problems during their sentence or they were reported as having no addiction problems. All of these factors were confirmed during interview to be indicators of low risk.

A forward date rather than parole was recommended in 19 cases. The main reason given for the forward date was to allow further time for testing or to begin/complete a period of counselling or training for freedom in custody.

As Table 8.2 indicates, in a small number of cases (4 or 6 per cent of positive outcomes) the reasons given for outcome related to negative aspects of the case: the prisoner was at a high risk of re-offending; had failed to address addiction problems; had made poor progress in custody and did not have any supportive relationships in the community to which they were to return. For these cases a forward date was recommended to provide an incentive to change and/or to allow further time for testing.

"-On balance .. if [he]had the incentive of a period [of parole] at the end, counselling might be more fruitful. Eight months forward date to allow drug counselling to continue and short period of parole."

(Transcript: Male prisoner, aged 28, serving short-term sentence for violent offences, considered to be potentially at high risk of re-offending with a drug addiction problem.)

Negative Outcomes: Early Review

In 27 cases the Board agreed to recommend an early review. The main reasons given for these decisions are summarised in Table 8.3.

Table 8.3: Non-Impact Cases: Reasons for Early Review

Context	Reason	Percent (n=27)	
Past Behaviour	Low No. Previous Convictions/1st Custodial	7	(2)
	High No. Previous Convictions	15	(4)
	Poor Response to Previous Supervision	7	(2)
	High Risk/Not Addressed Offending	67	(18)
	Psychological/Psychiatric Problems	7	(2)
Change in Custody	Addiction Problems	37	(10)
	Poor Conduct/Response to Testing	11	(3)
	Motivation to Change	56	(15)
	To Allow for Further Testing/Complete Training for Freedom	15	(4)
	To Complete Counselling/ Assess Progress	100	(27)
	Good Family Support	4	(1)
	Poor Family Support	15	(4)
Future Structures	Further Time to Clarify Plans (not linked to social work)	11	(3)
Other	Await Further Information	26	(7)

Percentages add up to more than 100 as more than one reason was given in most cases
Shaded areas: most frequently mentioned reasons
Numbers in brackets: actual number of cases

As the table indicates, all early review decisions were given in order that the Board could assess progress. Most cases had features which Parole Board interviewees confirmed to be indicators of high risk, for example the prisoner had not addressed their offending behaviour (18 or 67 per cent) or their addiction problems (10 or 37 per cent of these cases). However, for just over half of the cases the Board considered an early review to be appropriate because the prisoner had either made some efforts to tackle their problems or had given some indication that they were motivated to change.

"He's decided to seek alcohol counselling...six months early review to allow him to begin alcohol and anger control counselling - reports to the Parole Board on response. He's not addressed his offending."

(Transcript: Male prisoner aged 23, serving short-term sentence for violent offences, at first review with a period of less than one year available for parole.)

The primary focus of these cases was change in custody. Past behaviour and future structures were mentioned in only a minority of these decisions.

Negative Outcomes: Release not Recommended

In 56 of the non-impact determinate sentence cases the Board agreed not to recommend release. For most cases the principal reason given was that the prisoner had not addressed their offending behaviour and/or was at high risk of re-offending (mainly as a result of minimising their role in the offence). This was the only reason given for the decision in 19 (34 per cent) cases. Where risk of re-offending or failure to address addictions was not mentioned the reasons given for decisions always included either failure to address addictions or criminal history (or both). The main reasons given for decisions not to recommend release are summarised in Table 8.4. As the table indicates, almost all of the reasons given were confirmed by interviewees to be indicators of high risk.

Table: 8.4 Non-Impact Cases: Reasons for Recommendations not to Release

	Reason	Percent (n=56)	
Past Behaviour	High No. Previous Convictions	23	(13)
	Poor Response to Previous Supervision	13	(7)
	High Risk/Not Addressed Offending	88	(49)
Change in Custody	Addiction Problems	39	(22)
	Anger Management Problems	4	(2)
	Poor Conduct/Response to Testing	5	(3)
	Psychological/Psychiatric Problems	2	(1)
	Poor Family Support	11	(6)
Future Structures	Poor Accommodation	9	(5)
	Poor Likely Response to Supervision	4	(2)
Other	Await Further Information	2	(1)

Percentages do not add up to 100 as more than one reason was given for some cases
Shaded areas: most frequently mentioned reasons
Numbers in brackets: actual number of cases

Implications of Decision making Patterns

The decision making patterns indicate that risk of re-offending is the primary consideration in most non-impact cases. Positive outcomes were strongly associated with cases where prisoners had made steps to address their problems during time spent in custody and had supportive families to return to (low risk cases). By contrast, most prisoners who had failed to address their offending behaviour or addiction problems during time in custody (high risk cases) received negative outcomes. The only exceptions to this pattern were four cases with negative features which were recommended for a forward date to provide an incentive to change and/or to allow further time for testing. Release for these cases was conditional on progress being made.

These patterns confirm interviewees' perceptions that change in custody is one of the primary considerations in decision making. This highlights the limitations of a policy which is premised on the belief that reductions in the use of custody through earlier release on licence can be made by improving the quality and quantity of community based social work services. Where circumstances on release were given as reasons for outcome this was generally in respect of the quality of intra-familial relationships (as highlighted in Chapter Six this is a factor over which community based social work services may have little direct control). The focus on change in custody in these decisions does, however, highlight the potential for effective prison based social work services to impact on outcome.

For the policy to have greater impact on current practice, a shift would be required in the Board's perception of the stage in the criminal justice process at which risk can be most effectively reduced. Success for the policy could be claimed if the Board were prepared to release greater numbers of prisoners who had not made efforts to change in custody, in the expectation that community based social work services were better placed to effect behavioural change.

A key question remains, however, as to why social work services were found to be a crucial element in the 13 high risk cases in the impact sample (discussed in Chapter Seven) and less important for the other high risk cases in the non-impact sample. One explanation may be that the social work reports in the dossiers of the high risk cases in the non-impact sample did not indicate services which could be offered to prisoners on release. Unfortunately the number of relevant cases[48] in the report sample is too small (four cases) to test this explanation. In two cases in this sample services were offered to high risk non-impact cases not recommended for release, but in a further two cases services were not offered.

Another explanation may be the nature of the risk posed by these offenders. A number of the cases in the impact sample deemed to be high risk were potentially dangerous[49]: Again it is difficult to test this explanation.

---
[48] Relevant cases are non-impact cases which were not recommended for release by the Board because they were too high risk.

[49] Five of these cases were sex offenders which interviewees confirmed were the types of case over which they had most concerns. Two of the cases had mental health problems (this included one of the sex offenders) and were described during the presentation of the case to be potentially dangerous. One of the violent offenders in the sample was described as being a potential danger to his wife (the victim of the original offence).

Risk of danger was not mentioned in the non-impact high risk cases. Similarly the Board's concerns about risk and danger in relation to sex offenders did not extend to recommending the release of two other high risk sex offenders with short periods of parole available in the non-impact sample.

INDETERMINATE SENTENCE CASES

During the observation the Board considered the cases of 37 indeterminate sentence cases for which a provisional release recommendation was a potential outcome[50].

Characteristics of Cases

Life sentence prisoners differ in a number of important ways from determinate sentence cases. In addition to the seriousness of their offence, lifers will have served a much longer period in custody before they are reviewed by the Parole Board, than all but the most long-term determinate sentence prisoners. Additionally the life licence will be in place for the duration of the offender's natural life in contrast to the parole licence, which is terminated at the prisoner's two-thirds of sentence date.

Most of the lifers in the sample had served between nine and 15 years in custody with 13 (35 per cent) having served between nine and 11 years and 16 (43 per cent) between 12 and 15 years. Five cases (14 per cent) were at a review following a previous recall to custody with most others being at third or later review. Although a high proportion of the sample was referred for consideration of provisional release, ten (23 per cent) of these cases were referred for consideration of an adverse development (this type of referral is discussed in more detail at the end of the chapter). The characteristics of the sample are summarised in the following tables (other characteristics are described in more detail in Annex III).

Table 8.5: Lifers: Time Served

Served	Percent (n=37)	
6 - 8 Years	8	(3)
9 - 11 Years	35	(13)
12 - 15 Years	43	(16)
16+	14	(5)

Numbers in brackets: actual number of cases

Table 8.6: Lifers: Review Number

Review	Percent (n=36*)	
First	11	(4)
Second	17	(6)
Third or Later	58	(21)
Review Following Recall	14	(5)

* One case: information not available
Numbers in brackets: actual number of cases

---

[50] Five other indeterminate sentence cases were referred for the Board to note information. One of these cases was a child detained Without Limit of Time. The other four were cases where the Secretary of State had decided to insert additional requirements into the licence of a prisoner previously recommended for provisional release. The Board duly noted the information.
The cases of two life licencees were also referred to the Board for consideration of changes to their licence requirements. In one case the supervising officer had requested the removal of a residential requirement in the licence and in the other that a condition of alcohol counselling be amended. The Board agreed to the supervising officers' requests in both cases.

Outcomes

Almost two-thirds of indeterminate sentence cases received a positive outcome with ten (37 per cent) being recommended for a programme and six (22 per cent) for a formal referral at next review[51]. Eleven cases (41 per cent) were not recommended for provisional release at current review and the Board agreed to review these cases in one year's time.

The main reasons given for outcome confirm the views of Parole Board members that progress in custody is the key factor taken into account when making decisions on this type of case. The reasons for outcomes are summarised in the following table.

Table 8.7: Lifers: Reasons for Outcome

Reason	Programme Number (n=10)	Formal Referral Number (n=6)	Review In One Year Number (n=11)
Good Progress	9	3	2
Poor Conduct/Response to testing	-	-	4
Addressed Alcohol Problem	2	-	4
Addressed Mental Health Problems	1	-	-
Mental Health Problems	-	-	2
Not Addressed Offending	-	-	1
Incentive to Progress	-	2	-
Further Progress Required	-	-	4
Requirements of Justice Met	-	1	-

Numbers in some columns exceed total number of decisions as more than one reason for outcome was given.

As the table indicates, reasons given for endorsing the pre-release programmes and making a formal recommendation in favour of release (programme decisions), were all linked to progress in custody (in general) or to progress in addressing personal problems.

Good progress was again given as the key reason in half of the cases recommended for a formal referral at next review . A further supporting reason in one case was that the "requirements of justice had now been met". In two other cases the formal referral was recommended to provide the prisoner with an incentive to make progress.

For most cases not recommended for provisional release at current review, the main reasons given were poor conduct in custody and response to testing, and failure to address addiction problems. Other supporting reasons were failure to address mental health problems and failure to address offending. In two further cases, although the prisoner had made good progress they were, in the view of the Board, at too early a stage in their sentence for release to be considered.

> "If it weren't for positive reports, go with the [view of the] Trial Judge, but the dossier's positive. See in a year and if positives continued could put forward as exceptional circumstances case....Needs to progress through the system further."

> (Transcript: Male prisoner aged 27, period served: 10 years)

Implications of Decision making Patterns for Policy Implementation

The focus on progress and change in custody in decisions made on indeterminate sentence cases limits the potential for the National Standards and 100 per cent funding initiative to encourage the Parole Board to release such prisoners on licence at an earlier stage. (Most of the cases in the sample receiving positive outcomes were at third or later review and had spent between nine and 15 years in custody).

The key contributing factor in decision making may be the stage at which indeterminate sentence cases are referred to the Board for consideration of release. As highlighted above, two cases not recommended for

---

[51] A formal referral outcome was where the Board agreed to request that the case be re-referred to them at a later meeting as a "formal referral", that is at the next review, subject to the Secretary of State's authority to consult the judiciary, the Board would consider the provisional release date and pre-release programme as set out by the Department.

release had made good progress but were considered to be at too early a stage in their sentence for release to be a realistic option. Cases which receive a formal referral will spend perhaps a further year in custody before their case is returned to the Board for consideration of the pre-release programme. Detailed considerations of release plans might therefore be inappropriate at this stage.

Where cases are referred to the Board with a pre-release programme, release from custody may again be at least a year away and conditional upon successful completion of the programme. The pre-release programmes which the cases in the sample were given only included plans for the prisoner's remaining period in custody (the most common programme being six months training for freedom and six months in open conditions). In a number of the prison social work reports in the sample, the authors commented that detailed planning for release would only begin once the prisoner had been given a pre-release programme.

The focus on progress, however, does suggest that there is greater potential for prison social work services to impact on decision making. The most frequently mentioned indicator of progress was whether the prisoner had addressed their underlying problems. *Continuity Through Co-operation* states that a key task of prison social work is to assess prisoners' social and personal needs and to work with prisoners and their families to assist eventual resettlement in the community. However, progress is also dependent on the opportunities which are available for testing and this can be inhibited as much by administrative arrangements within prison establishments and by Scottish Prison Service policies on security classifications, as by the behaviour of individual prisoners.

ADVERSE DEVELOPMENTS

As highlighted above, 12 determinate and ten indeterminate sentence cases were referred for an adverse development[52]. This was where the prisoner had either been recommended for (provisional) release but had been given a misconduct report or had allegedly committed a further offence prior to release.

Outcomes

The decisions made in cases referred for an adverse development provide further evidence for the argument that the potential for community based social work services to impact on decision making may be dependent upon the stage at which a case is referred to the Board.

The outcomes of these cases were directly related to the seriousness with which the alleged incident was viewed by the Board. The outcomes are summarised in the following table.

Table 8.8: Adverse Developments: Outcome

Outcome	Percent (n=22)
Withdraw Date	45 (10)
Continuation	27 (6)
Retain Date	18 (4)
Defer Date	9 (2)

Percentages do not add up to 100 because of rounding
Numbers in brackets: actual number of cases

Dates were withdrawn where the prisoner was considered to have grossly abused trust (for example by smuggling drugs into custody after being on home leave). Where the release date was allowed to stand the breach of trust was considered to be minimal (for example, a case where the prisoner had allegedly stolen food from a hot-plate).

In a number of cases which had received a misconduct report the Board agreed to defer the release date, the length of deferral matching the length of punishment given by the governor. Other cases were continued for further information about the incident or to await the outcome of the trial (in cases where further charges had been brought against the prisoner).

---

[52] Seven other cases which had previously been recommended for parole or a provisional release date were re-referred during the fieldwork period because of an adverse development. The decision making patterns in these cases reflect those described above.

SUMMARY

The decision making patterns in respect of non-impact and indeterminate sentence cases confirm the views of Parole Board members that risk of re-offending (for determinate sentence cases) and progress in custody (for indeterminate sentence cases) are the key factors determining outcome. The importance of these criteria will limit the impact of a policy which aims to encourage earlier release on licence by improving the quality and quantity of community based social work services. For most determinate sentence cases, greater policy impact would require a shift in the Board's perspective on the context in which risk can be most effectively reduced. However, for indeterminate sentence cases an impediment to policy impact may be the stage at which these cases are referred to the Board. Release on licence for most indeterminate sentence cases will be at least one year away from the time at which the case is considered by the Board and dependent upon the successful completion of a pre-release programme. Detailed planning for release may not begin until the prisoner has been recommended for provisional release (as confirmed in a number of prison social work reports for indeterminate sentence cases in the sample).

PART 3

BREACH AND RECALL

CHAPTER NINE

BREACH AND RECALL

INTRODUCTION

The National Standards state that one of the main objectives of statutory supervision is to ensure that offenders adhere to their licence conditions. They set out detailed guidance for social workers on the procedures to be followed when offenders are in breach of their licence.

This chapter explores Parole Board and social work views on breach procedures and the relationship between breaches of licence and the quality of social work supervision; examines the factors which the Board takes into account in practice when making decisions on this type of case; and considers the implications of the decision making patterns for successful policy implementation.

IMPACT OF STANDARDS ON BREACH PROCEDURES

There was consensus amongst most Parole Board interviewees that they had not been aware of any changes in breach procedures since the implementation of the policy. However, breach procedures were considered to be generally satisfactory.

Community based social workers commented that since the implementation of the National Standards breach procedures had worked better. However, they considered that this was due to a change in the practice of Central Government. A number commented that in the past they had sent in reports of breaches to The Scottish Office Home Department (the Department) and nothing had been done. Now when they reported a breach to the Department every report was immediately followed up.

RELATIONSHIP BETWEEN QUALITY OF SUPERVISION AND BREACH

Parole Board Views

Parole Board interviewees were equivocal about whether the quality of supervision could impact on breaches of licence. Most cases which were referred to the Board for consideration of recall were cases where the licencee had been charged with, or convicted of further offences. Whilst high quality supervision was considered to assist licencees to adhere to the conditions of their licence, a general view was that there was little social work could do to prevent re-offending.

> "I suppose the efficiency of supervision must be connected (with breach) but they'll re-offend if they're going to and there's nothing that social work can do about it." (Parole Board Member)

This contrasts with the model of social work practice in the National Standards which is premised on the view that supervision which provides the requisite balance of care and control can impact positively on offending behaviour.

Community based Social Work Views

Community based social work interviewees linked breaches of licences less to the quality of social work services in assisting licencees to address their offending, and more to the breakdown of practical arrangements (for example where accommodation arrangements fell through or the licencee got into financial difficulties).

> "If they're going to breach they'll do it in the first three months. You've got to get them through the transitional period. Shelter, food, money..if you haven't dealt with them you're onto a loser. You can't possibly expect to supervise someone of no fixed abode and who's skint." (Community based Social Worker)

Interviewees commented that release arrangements were vulnerable to breaking down because of poor co-ordination between prison based and community based social workers. The National Standards state that following notification of a release date the prison based social worker, the supervising social worker in the community and the prisoner should draw up a statement identifying and assessing the prisoner's needs and outlining detailed pre- and post-release plans[53]. However, community based social work interviewees commented that this three way meeting did not take place as often as it should because of time constraints. A number of licencees were therefore being released without this detailed planning. Difficulties in this regard were compounded because community based social workers were often not informed about the outcome of cases for which they had prepared a home circumstances report.

The National Standards state that failures to comply with licence requirements during the first three months of a licence should be regarded particularly seriously. A number of community based social workers interviewed commented that the Standards were too prescriptive in this respect. Because the transition from prison to the community was a particularly difficult one and because newly released prisoners were especially vulnerable, supervising officers should be more *lenient* with licencees in the early stages of supervision.

> "There needs to be a cooling off period in the first three months if they don't turn up for appointments. There's a need for a space for a relationship to be established without .... saying if you don't turn up it's a written warning. Firmness during this period but not rigidity." (Community based Social Worker)

PERCEPTIONS OF DECISION MAKING

Parole Board interviewees stated that the main factor which they took into consideration in recall cases was risk, both in respect of re-offending and whether or not the offender was a danger to the public.

> "What I think about is whether the risk of continuing supervision is too high to be sustained." (Parole Board Member)

> "Risk of re-offending that's the main one and what level of risk that re-offending poses [to the public]." (Parole Board Member)

Interviewees commented that they found cases in which the licencee had been charged with further offences the most difficult to deal with as they were required to balance the rights of the accused with an assessment of the level of risk which the licencee posed.

A number of Parole Board interviewees commented that they often received reports from supervising officers which stated that the licencee had been charged with further offences but without clarifying the circumstances surrounding the alleged offence or whether the licencee's behaviour was giving cause for concern.

> "It is the expectation of the Board that people will report to us behaviour that is adverse for want of a better word. It poses all sorts of dilemmas when people write to us saying only he's been charged with breach of the peace. What do we do about it? It's the behaviour surrounding the alleged offence which might give us cause for concern as opposed to just writing to us to say that an offence has been committed." (Parole Board Member)

A key concern of Parole Board interviewees, however, was to support supervising officers by reinforcing the seriousness with which licencees should treat parole or release on life licence. A common view was that supervising officers only report cases to the Department where there have been a number of breaches. Any cases referred for consideration of recall were therefore perceived to be fairly serious breaches.

DECISION MAKING PRACTICE

During the observation the cases of 47 licencees were referred to the Board for consideration of recall. The sample comprises: 20 life licencees; 11 young people subject to statutory aftercare licences and 15 parolees[54]. (The main characteristics of this sample are described in more detail in Annex III).

Types of Referral

The recall cases comprised four main types of referral: charged cases where the licence had been charged with further offences but the case had not yet come to trial (27 cases); convicted cases where the offender had been found guilty of further offences (6 cases); non-convicted cases where the charges against the licencee had been dropped or where the licencee had been found not guilty (9 cases); and breach cases where the licencee had failed to comply with other licence requirements (3 cases). In one other case the licencee had requested a return to custody.

---

[53] *National Objectives and Standards:* Throughcare Paragraph 52.
[54] One further case was referred because of the death of the licencee and therefore the characteristics of this case will not be included in the description of the sample nor in the examination of decision making patterns.

Outcomes

The types of outcome and reasons given for recall cases are described in the following table.

Table 9.1: Recall Cases: Reasons for Outcome

Reason	Recall Number (n=13)	Change Reporting Number (n=8)	Warning Letter Number (n=3)	No Change Number (n=3)	Continue Case Number (n=19)
Risk of Re-Offending	5	4	-	-	-
Public Danger	7	-	-	-	-
Addiction Problems	4	1	-	-	-
Poor Response to Supervision/ Behaviour Giving Cause for Concern	3	3	1	-	-
Good Response to Supervision	-	-	1	3	-
High Tariff Court Disposal	3	-	-	-	-
Low Tariff Court Disposal/ Minor Charge	-	-	1	1	-
Not Informed Supervising Officer of Charges	-	1	1	-	-
Undesirable Associates	-	1	-	-	-
Await Outcome of Trial	-	-	-	-	15
Await Information about Response to Supervision	-	-	-	-	4

Numbers in some columns exceed total number of cases as more than one reason was given in some cases

Consideration of risk permeates most of the decision making patterns in relation to recall cases. The reasons given for outcome focused for the most part on risk or on factors which were confirmed in interview to be risk indicators (for example addiction problems). Risk in the context of recall cases was more explicitly linked to concerns about danger and public safety than it was in decisions made on other types of case. Key factors indicating danger were poor response to supervision and violent behaviour, especially where the licencee had a history of violent offences. Even in cases where charges had been dropped against such licencees the Board took steps to ensure that the licencee's behaviour was monitored more carefully (through increased reporting frequency).

The decision making patterns suggest that where the Board has to weigh up the risks of continuing supervision with considerations of public safety, in most cases the latter takes precedence. This even occurred in the small number of cases (2) where social workers indicated services which they could offer to enable supervision in the community to continue. Good response to supervision was only given as a reason for outcome in cases where either the licencee had been found not guilty of minor offences or where a probation order had been given and the licencee was now under stricter control.

The main type of case which the Board was required to deal with during the observation were charged cases. These were cases which the Board identified in interview as being the most difficult type of case on which to take a decision. The National Standards state that supervising officers must report a case to the Department where a licencee has been convicted for further offences. Although there is also a requirement for supervising officers to report behaviour which constitutes a serious risk to the community, they are not required to report a case where the licencee has been charged with further offences and the case has not yet gone to trial. These cases present particular difficulties because the Board is required to balance the individual rights of the licencee against concerns for community protection. Social workers do not have any detailed guidance about the circumstances in which it would be appropriate to report charged cases nor about how public danger should be assessed. Although assessments of danger would appear relatively straightforward to make in cases where a licencee has been charged with assault, other types of incident are less clear cut. For example how should a social worker assess the danger posed by a licencee who had been charged with house-breaking? A number of the community based social workers interviewed commented that they were very inexperienced in supervising parolees and life licencees (having to deal with around one case per year or less) and that clearer guidelines would enhance their confidence in dealing with charged cases.

SUMMARY

Although Parole Board interviewees had not discerned any changes in the quality of breach procedures since policy implementation they were generally satisfied with the way in which current arrangements operated. Social workers, however, considered that The Scottish Office Home Department was now more assiduous in processing cases which they reported for breach of licence.

Interviewees were equivocal as to whether there was a relationship between breaches of licence and quality of supervision. Parole Board interviewees considered that quality of supervision was likely to impact on licencees' willingness to adhere to their licence conditions; however they considered that there was little that social workers could do to prevent re-offending. Social workers were of the view that breaches were more likely to occur when practical arrangements broke down. A key concern was poor co-ordination between prison and community based social workers over release arrangements.

The main focus of the recall decision was the nature of the alleged breach and the extent to which it indicated an increased risk of re-offending or heightened level of danger. It would appear that services which social work can offer to enable supervision to continue are only likely to be a secondary consideration, and only in a minority of cases (where the alleged breach is extremely minor or where charges have been dropped against the licencee). Reporting a case generally resulted in increased control of the licencee (either through recall or increased reporting frequency) even in cases where charges had been dropped or the licencee had been found not guilty of further offences. Information provided by supervising officers was, however, perceived to be crucial to decision making, as progress on supervision was a key element in the risk of danger assessment. Although the National Standards include detailed guidance on making assessment of risk of re-offending, there is little detailed guidance for social workers on making assessments of danger.

CHAPTER TEN

CONCLUSION

IMPACT OF ARRANGEMENTS FOR POLICY IMPLEMENTATION ON DECISION MAKING

The analysis of the decision making patterns has indicated that assessments of risk have an important role to play in the decisions made on determinate sentence cases referred for consideration of release and recall cases. For determinate sentence cases risk was associated with risk of re-offending. However, for cases referred for consideration of recall, risk was more explicitly linked to public danger. The way in which risk was assessed by the Board places limitations on the ability of the policy to impact on decision making.

Key elements of the risk assessment were identified by Parole Board interviewees as: criminal history; efforts made to address offending and other underlying problems during time spent in custody; the quality of family relationships; and constructive release plans. However, the decision making patterns indicate that in the majority of cases where the Board considers that a prisoner has not made efforts to address their offending or where a licencee's behaviour is giving cause for concern, the Board attaches less weight to constructive release plans in their assessment of risk. Where the Parole Board perceives a prisoner to be low risk they recommend them for parole or a forward release date. High risk prisoners by contrast are generally not released.

Parole Board interviewees did not consider that arrangements for implementing the policy had impacted on their decision-making practice. However, they did indicate that community based social work services could have a key role to play in decisions to release a small number of high risk prisoners for a short period of parole. The aim of the Board in releasing these prisoners on licence was that they would return to a controlled environment. The role of social work under these circumstances is less rehabilitative and more a means of keeping track of offenders.

Analysis of the decision making patterns identified 39 cases out of 253 for which there was evidence that social work services were an important consideration in the decision that was made. However, a high proportion of these cases was considered to be at a low risk of re-offending by the Board or had features which the Board confirmed in interview to be indicative of a low risk of re-offending. This suggests that the availability of social work services did not have a pivotal role to play in the decisions made to recommend early release, as all low risk cases during the observation received positive outcomes. However, in 13 high risk and potentially dangerous cases (mainly convicted of violent and sex offences) the availability of social work services was a crucial element in the decision made. Although a policy aim is to enable more serious offenders to be dealt with in a community based setting, it is difficult to conclude that the positive outcomes associated with some of these cases represent a major success for the policy. If the policy were impacting on decision making one would expect to find a greater number of high risk cases being recommended for release.

For indeterminate sentence prisoners the principal focus of decision making was progress in custody. The focus on this criterion limits the impact a policy can have which aims to encourage earlier release by targeting the community based element of throughcare services. A further impediment to policy impact may be the stage at which these case are referred to the Board. Release on licence for most indeterminate sentence cases will be at least one year away from the time at which the case is considered by the Board and dependent upon the successful completion of a pre-release programme. Detailed planning for release may not begin until the prisoner has been recommended for provisional release (as confirmed in a number of prison social work reports for indeterminate sentence cases in the report sample).

The focus on change during time spent in custody (both in respect of progress for indeterminate sentence cases and reduction in the level of risk for determinate sentence cases) highlights the scope for high quality and effective prison based social work to impact positively on parole decisions. For community based social work to have greater impact would require a shift in the Board's views on the context in which changes in behaviour and attitudes can be best effected. When asked about factors impacting on breach a general view was that there was little that community based social work services could do to prevent re-offending.

Parole Board members do not generally receive feedback on the progress of parole supervision other than where a case has been referred for consideration of recall. More detailed information about the effectiveness of supervision and specialist community based programmes might encourage the Board to reconsider their views on the role which community based social work resources can play in risk reduction.

Relationship Between Social Work Reports and Parole Decisions

Parole Board interviewees looked to prison social work reports to provide information about release plans, progress in custody and an assessment of risk. Home circumstances reports were also cited as a valuable source of information on these factors in addition to providing information on the suitability of the release address. When making decisions on individual cases it is the practice of the Board to consider all reports in the parole dossier and to compare and contrast the assessments provided by social workers with other accounts. This was considered to limit the impact which individual reports could have on decisions made.

Most of the reports in the sample did not provide the types of assessment which the Board looked for in these reports. None of the prison social work reports provided all of the assessments required by National Standards and only five percent of home circumstances reports did so. Lack of relevant assessments is likely to inhibit the impact which information provided by social work can have on decision making. Social work interviewee responses indicate, however, that social workers often do not have ready access to relevant information which would enable them to make assessments. Most found it difficult, for example, to access information about the prisoner's criminal history in order to make an assessment of risk. Importantly both prison social workers and community based social workers identified elements of reports which each considered that the other should take primary responsibility for. The development of release plans was one such element. Prison social workers did not consider that they were best placed to assess the suitability of community based resources for the prisoner, whereas community based social workers did not consider that they had sufficient information about the prisoner in order to assess their needs.

There were variations in view about the impact of National Standards on report writing. Some interviewees considered that improved quality of reports was attributable to the policy, others that quality was more associated with the ability of individual social workers. Although most of the reports in our sample did not meet National Standards requirements, during the observation poor quality of information provided by social workers was only a factor in a minority of cases.

Quality of Prison Social Work Services

As highlighted above, the focus on addressing offending and other underlying problems in decision making suggests that the services which prison social work provides can impact positively on parole decisions. The Parole Board did consider that prison social workers were generally effective in assisting prisoners to address their offending but highlighted a number of inhibiting factors. Firstly, prisoners themselves had to be motivated to change and the most high risk prisoners tended to be the least tractable. Secondly, the prison social work role was considered to be more effective when a network of services was available in individual establishments (including specialist drug and alcohol counselling services and psychological services). A common concern of interviewees was that there was little consistency in the types of services provided in different prison establishments.

There were variations in view as to whether there had been improvements in the quality of prison social work services since the implementation of *Continuity Through Co-operation*. While it was generally recognised that social workers were now undertaking more offence focused work, a lack of a strategic approach to service development and the workloads of some social workers were considered to have hampered the range and effectiveness of services in some establishments.

Quality of Community Based Services

Interviewee responses indicate that although policy implementation has led to proliferation of certain services (especially drug and alcohol counselling services) significant gaps remain. Accommodation was identified by almost all interviewees as a key area requiring further development. The decision making patterns indicate, however, that demand for supported accommodation (as evidenced by additional licence requirements) is relatively low. By contrast, areas for which there is the greatest demand, for example alcohol counselling, are the best served.

THE IMPACT OF LIAISON ON PAROLE BOARD DECISION MAKING

When asked about liaison Parole Board members had little to say. Liaison between the Parole Board and officials from SWSG and SPS generally took place when officials attended the Parole Board's General Purposes meetings. While some were satisfied with these arrangements others felt that the Board required to be consulted more often about the development of policy.

Importantly the Board appeared to lack information about available services and specialist programmes which would assist their decision making, with one interviewee commenting that they often had to rely on individual Board members, who were the representatives from social work and the prison services, to give them information about key developments.

Good inter- and intra-agency co-ordination were found to be a key element in the preparation of high quality social work reports and in the provision of effective prison and community based social work supervision. Interviewee responses indicate that arrangements did not always work well. A particular concern was the poor co-ordination of release arrangements between prison social workers and community based social workers. Social workers attributed difficulties both to time constraints and to a lack of clear information about when prisoners were being released. A common view amongst community based social workers was that they lacked feedback on parole decisions.

Throughcare services were identified at Phase One of the research programme as being the most poorly developed element of social work criminal justice services. Interviewee responses indicate that the aspects of throughcare which impact on parole decision making are still unevenly developed. Improving the quality of services, however, is not likely to facilitate earlier release on licence for more serious and persistent offenders without a corresponding change in the Board's views on the context in which risk reduction can best take place. A key aim of Central Government is to facilitate common ownership of the policy in order that key criminal justice decision makers develop shared perspectives on the role of social work in risk management. Liaison is considered to have a key role to play in this. It would appear from the research findings of this study that common ownership does not as yet extend to the Parole Board.

ANNEX I

PAROLE PROCEDURES

DETERMINATE SENTENCE CASES

Prior to the implementation of the Prisoners and Criminal Proceedings (Scotland) Act 1993, prisoners serving determinate sentences of imprisonment or of detention in a Young Offenders' Institution were eligible for release on parole after completing a third of sentence (Parole Qualifying Date or PQD) or one year whichever was longer. In practice this meant that only prisoners serving periods of 18 months or more would come into the parole system. Prisoners were not obliged to be considered for parole and could opt out of the process.

Cases under the old arrangements were initially reviewed by the Local Review Committee (LRC)[55] and it would make a recommendation to the Secretary of State. In practice if parole was recommended the cases would be referred directly to the Parole Board[56]. Where parole was not recommended for adult male prisoners officials from The Scottish Office Home Department (the Department) would examine the case using a system of prediction scoring[57]. Cases which received a favourable score would be referred to the Board. The cases of women and young offenders were considered by a "Sift Committee" (normally comprising two officials from the Department). If they passed this Committee they would be referred to the Board. Cases which did not receive a favourable prediction score or who did not pass the Sift Committee were refused parole but their cases would be eligible for review again in one year.

INDETERMINATE SENTENCE CASES

Arrangements for reviewing indeterminate sentence cases have also recently been changed as a result of the implementation of the Prisoners and Criminal Proceedings (Scotland) Act 1993 and a subsequent review by the then Secretary of State.

Under the old arrangements both mandatory and discretionary life sentence cases were first considered by the Preliminary Review Committee with a view to recommending a date to the Secretary of State for the prisoner's first formal review of their suitability for release on life licence. This usually occurred around four years into their sentence. The Department would then write to the prison to initiate the first review about two months prior to the date approved by the Secretary of State. The prisoner would be interviewed by a member of the LRC. If the LRC recommended the granting of a provisional release date and the Department agreed, the Secretary of State would refer the case to the Lord Justice General, the trial judge (where available) and to the Parole Board. In cases where the Secretary of State did not authorise consultation with the judiciary the case would be referred to the Parole Board for information with a proposal for a later review.

If the LRC did not recommend release or if the Department disagreed with their recommendation the case would be referred to the Parole Board for information. If the Board disagreed with either the LRC or Department's view that a provisional release date would not be appropriate, the Board would request that the Secretary of State initiate consultation with the judiciary. Where the LRC were in favour of release but the Department considered the case to be particularly complex then the case could be referred to the Board for preliminary consultation prior to being referred to the Secretary of State.

RECALL CASES

Parolees and life licencees are liable to recall to custody if they fail to comply with the conditions of their licence or commit a further offence. The revocation of a licence is formally the prerogative of the Secretary of

---

[55] Local Review Committees were set up under the Criminal Justice Act 1967 to review cases eligible for release under the Act and to interview such prisoners. A LRC is appointed by the Secretary of State for each penal institution. It comprises at minimum the Governor of the establishment (or their representative); a social worker and an independent member. LRCs were abolished under the new arrangements introduced by the Prisoners and Criminal Proceedings (Scotland) Act 1993 .

[56] The main exceptions to this were cases covered by the "1984 Statement". The 1984 Statement, made by the then Secretary of State on 18 December 1984, states that the Secretary of State would be reluctant to authorise the release, except in exceptional circumstances, of any persons serving five years or more for violent crimes or drug trafficking. The other exception is prisoners convicted of terrorist offences. Any case in such groups would not normally be prepared for parole and would be referred to the Board for information.

[57] Prediction scoring is a method for assessing risk of re-offending. The method used by the Department was developed at the University of Edinburgh and is based on six factors including age and previous convictions.

State but he is required to consult the Parole Board beforehand. In certain cases, if the grounds are sufficiently serious the Department may implement a "Secretary of State's Recall" and the individual will be returned to custody before their case has been referred to the Board. Once an individual has been recalled they have the right to written representations (and formerly an interview with the Local Review Committee). The Board may then decide on the basis of this information and the circumstances of the case to order the immediate re-release of the individual concerned. Recalled parolees remain in prison until their two-thirds of sentence date or until a later successful parole application, whilst recalled life licencees remain in prison until the Board recommends re-release. Other options are available to the Board in cases referred for consideration of recall (recall cases) for example: the Board may agree to vary the conditions of the parole or life licence; to increase the reporting frequency; to send a warning letter to the licencee, or do nothing.

PRISONERS AND CRIMINAL PROCEEDINGS (SCOTLAND) ACT 1993

- The key changes introduced by this Act which relate to Parole are:

- Statutory after-care licences abolished;

- Unconditional release at half sentence for prisoners serving under four years (short term sentences);

- Option of Supervised Release Order for those serving between 12 months and four years: imposed at point of sentence;

- Prisoners serving four years or over, Parole Qualifying Date at one half of sentence; parole licence expires at end of sentence;

- Prisoners not granted parole: release under licence at two-thirds of sentence date: licence remains in force until end of sentence.

ANNEX II

METHODS

OBSERVATION

During the observation of the Parole Board meetings detailed transcripts (as near as possible verbatim) were taken of the presentations, discussions and reasons given for individual decisions.

In order to assess the current impact of social work services on decision making a detailed examination was undertaken of the relationship between parole decisions and a number of key factors including: the characteristics of the prisoner and the offence; length of prison term; extent to which prisoner had made use of prison social work or other services and progress made; provisional release package (where applicable) and circumstances on release.

ANALYSIS OF REPORT DATA

In order to assess the relationship between the quality of information provided by social workers (as measured by the extent to which reports met the National Standards) and Parole Board decisions, a sample of dossiers from cases considered at the meetings was drawn for more detailed analysis. The dossiers were those of all cases from each of the four study prison units (selected to cover the range of case categories with which the Board deals). The prison social work and home circumstances reports were extracted from these dossiers. These reports were examined to assess the extent to which they met National Standards and the Parole Board's requirements for information. The following information was also extracted from these reports and examined in relation to the outcome of cases: provisional release package; and social work assessments relevant to the report under consideration (including progress in custody; assessments of risk of further offending; and the social and family context to which the prisoner would return).

INTERVIEWS

Semi-structured interviews were conducted with four members of the Parole Board for Scotland and four prison social workers, one from each of the study prison units. In addition four group interviews were conducted with social workers from offender services teams in each of the study sites.

All interviewees were asked to comment on the decision making patterns identified during the observation. Interviewees were also asked about areas of concern specific to their role in the parole process.

Parole Board members were asked about:

- their aims in making decisions to release prisoners on licence;
- the impact of national standards on prison social work and home circumstances reports;
- views on the quality of prison based social work services and the impact of these on decision making;
- the impact of the policy on the quality of community based social work services and the relationship between services which social work can offer and parole decisions.
- formal and informal liaison arrangements between the Parole Board, local authorities and Central Government and their impact on decision making.

Prison social workers were asked about:

- the preparation of prison social work reports;
- the impact of *Continuity Through Co-operation* on prison social work services.

Community based social workers were asked to comment on:

- the preparation of home circumstances reports;
- the impact of the policy on services for and supervision of released prisoners.

ANNEX III

CHARACTERISTICS OF SAMPLES

During the observation the Board considered 311 cases. A number of cases were referred on more than one occasion and therefore the total number of decisions (n=345) exceeds the number of cases.

IMPACT SAMPLE CHARACTERISTICS

There were 39 cases in the main observation sample where there was evidence that social work had impacted on outcome. All but one of these cases were male.

Table 1: Impact cases: Offence

Offence	Percent (n=39)
Violence	56 (22)
Sex	21 (8)
Misuse of Drugs Act	13 (5)
Dishonesty	8 (3)
Road Traffic Act	3 (1)

Percentages do not add up to 100 because of rounding
Numbers in brackets: actual number of cases

Table 2: Impact Cases: Age

Age	Percent (n=39)
16 - 20	8 (3)
21 - 30	46 (18)
31 - 40	36 (14)
41+	10 (4)

Numbers in brackets: actual number of cases

Table 3: Impact cases: Current Sentence

Current Sentencec	Percent (n=39)
Less Than 4 Years	33 (13)
4 + Years	67 (26)

Numbers in brackets: actual number of cases

Table 4: Impact cases: Review Number

Review Number	Percent (n=39)
First	38 (15)
Second	31 (12)
Third Or Later	31 (12)

Numbers in brackets: actual number of cases

Table 5: Impact cases: Parole Available

Parole Available	Percent (n=39)
Less Than 1 Year	72 (28)
1 Year +	28 (11)

NON-IMPACT SAMPLE: CHARACTERISTICS

There were 177 determinate sentence cases where consideration of social work services did not feature in the reasons given by the Board for outcome. All but two of these cases were male.

Table 6: NonImpact cases: Offence Type

Offence	Percent (n=177)
Violence	63 (112)
Sex	8 (15)
Misuse of Drugs Act	18 (31)
Dishonesty	8 (14)
Other	3 (5)

Table 7: Non-Impact: Age

Age	Percent (n=39)
16 - 20	8 (14)
21 - 30	52 (92)
31 - 40	27 (48)
41+	13 (23)

Numbers in brackets: actual number of cases

Table 8: Non-Impact: Current Sentence

Current Sentencec	Percent (n=177)
Less Than 4 Years	42 (75)
4 + Years	58 (102)

Numbers in brackets: actual number of cases

Table 9: Non-Impact: Review Number

Review Number	Percent (n=177)
First	60 (107)
Second	29 (52)
Third Or Later	10 (18)

Percentages do not add up to 100 because of rounding
Numbers in brackets: actual number of cases

Table 10: Non-Impact cases: Parole Available

Parole Available	Percent (n=177)
Less Than 1 Year	55 (98)
1 Year +	45 (79)

Numbers in brackets: actual number of cases

INDETERMINATE SENTENCE CASES: CHARACTERISTICS

The Board considered the cases of 37 indeterminate sentence cases for which a provisional release recommendation was a potential outcome. All but one of the sample were male.

Table 11: Indeterminate Sentence Cases: Age

Age	Percent (n=37)
21 - 30 Years	22 (8)
31 - 40 Years	59 (22)
41+	19 (7)

Numbers in brackets: actual number of cases

Table 12: Indeterminate Sentence Cases: Time Served

Served	Percent (n=37)
6 - 8 Years	8 (3)
9 - 11 Years	35(13)
12 - 15 Years	43 (16)
16+	14 (5)

Numbers in brackets: actual number of cases

Table 13: Indeterminate Sentence Cases: Review Number

Review Number	Percent (n=36*)
First	11 (4)
Second	17 (6)
Third or Later	58 (21)
Review Following Recall	14 (5)

* 1 case: information not available
Numbers in brackets: actual number of cases

RECALL CASES: CHARACTERISTICS

During the observation the Board considered the cases of 47 licencees who were referred for consideration of recall. (In one of these cases the licencee had died and therefore their characteristics are not included in the following description of the recall sample). The sample comprises 20 life licencees, 11 young people subject to statutory supervision and 15 parolees.

All the recall cases were male.

Table 14: Recall Cases: Age

Age	Percent (n=46)
16 - 20	22 (10)
21 - 30	22 (10)
31 - 40	33 (15)
41+	24 (11)

Percentages do not add up to 100 because of rounding
Numbers in brackets: actual number of cases

Table 15: Recall Cases: Type of Referral

Type Of Referral	Percent (n=39)
Charged Cases	59 (27)
Convicted Cases	13 (6)
Non-Convicted Cases	20 (9)
Breach Cases	7 (3)
Request Return to Custody	2 (1)

Percentages do not add up to 100 because of rounding
Numbers in brackets: actual number of cases

Over half of the sample were referred for consideration of recall during the first six months of their licence with 15 (33 per cent) being referred during the first three months and a further nine (20 per cent) referred between four and six months. All of these cases were either parolees or statutory aftercare cases. All life licencees (with the exception of one case which was referred after the licencee had spent a period of 11 months on licence), were referred after a period of at least two years on licence. Of these eight (17 per cent of the whole sample of recall cases) had been on licence for periods of between two and five years with a further 11 cases (24 per cent of the whole sample of recall cases) having been on licence for periods of six years or more.

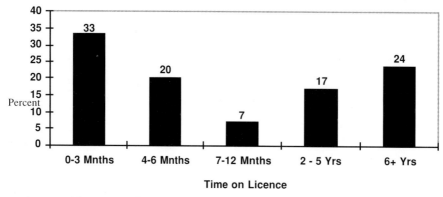

Figure 1: Recall Cases: Length of Time on Licence

Percentages do not add up to 100 because of rounding

68

REFERENCES

Brown, L. and Levy, L. (1998) *Social Work and Criminal Justice: Sentencer Decision Making.* Edinburgh: The Stationery Office.

Brown, L., Levy, L. and McIvor, G. (1998) *Social Work and Criminal Justice: The National and Local Context.* Edinburgh: The Stationery Office.

Hood, R. and Shute, S. (1994) *Parole in Transition. Evaluating the Impact and Effectiveness of Changes in the Parole System: Phase One.* Occasional Paper No. 13, Oxford: Centre for Criminological Research.

Maguire, M. in Stockdale, E. and Casale, S. eds. (1992) *Criminal Justice Under Stress.* London: Blackstone Press.

McAra, L. (1998) *Social Work and Criminal Justice: Early Arrangements.* Edinburgh: The Stationery Office.

McIvor, G. and Barry, M. (1998a) *Social Work and Criminal Justice: Probation.* Edinburgh: The Stationery Office.

McIvor, G. and Barry, M. (1998a) *Social Work and Criminal Justice: Community Based Throughcare.* Edinburgh: The Stationery Office.

Morris, P. and Beverly, F. (1975) *On Licence: A Study of Parole.* London: John Wiley.

Nuttall, C.P. et al. (1977) *Parole in England and Wales.* London: HMSO.

Paterson, F. and Tombs, J. (1998) *Social Work and Criminal Justice: The Impact of Policy:* Edinburgh: The Stationery Office.

Report of the Review Committee, Chairman: The Honourable Lord Kincraig (1989) *Parole and Related Issues in Scotland.* Edinburgh: HMSO.

Prisoners and Criminal Proceedings (Scotland) Act 1993.

Scottish Prison Service (1990) *Opportunity and Responsibility.* Edinburgh: HMSO.

Social Work Services Group (1991) *National Objectives and Standards for Social Work Services in the Criminal Justice System.* Edinburgh: The Scottish Office.

The Scottish Office Social Work Services Group/Scottish Prison Service (1989) *Continuity Through Co-operation.* Edinburgh: HMSO.

Ward, D. (1987) *The Validity of the Reconviction Prediction Score.* London: HMSO.

Printed in Scotland for The Stationery Office Limited
J37711, C7, 2/98, CCN 003808